INTRODUCING ENGLISH FOR RESEARCH PUBLICATION PURPOSES

There has been growing scholarly research and interest in writing for academic publication over the past decade and the field of English for Research Publication Purposes (ERPP) has established itself as an important domain within English for Academic Purposes (EAP). This introductory volume provides a comprehensive view of what ERPP encompasses as a scholarly field, including its disciplinary boundaries, competing discourses within the field, research and practice paradigms, and future prospects for research and pedagogy in this field.

The book portrays a multifaceted and nuanced picture of the discourses and discussions shaping and underlying ERPP, focusing on key aspects including:

- emergence and expansion of ERPP;
- key theoretical and methodological orientations framing ERPP research;
- writing for scholarly publication practices of EAL, Anglophone, and early-career scholars and graduate students;
- the pedagogy of ERPP and relevant international policies, practices, and initiatives;
- the advancement of digital technologies and the implications for ERPP;
- new directions in ERPP practice and research.

This book is essential reading for students and scholars within the areas of applied linguistics, TESOL, and English for Academic Purposes.

John Flowerdew is a Visiting Chair at the University of Lancaster and a Visiting Research Fellow at Birkbeck, University of London. He was previously a Professor at City University of Hong Kong and at the University of Leeds.

Pejman Habibie is an Assistant Professor of TESOL & Applied Linguistics at Western University, Canada. His research interests include EAP, writing for scholarly publication, and academic literacies. He is also a founding co-editor of the *Journal of English for Research Publication Purposes*.

INTRODUCING ENGLISH FOR RESEARCH PUBLICATION PURPOSES

John Flowerdew and Pejman Habibie

LONDON AND NEW YORK

First published 2022
by Routledge
2 Park Square, Milton Park, Abingdon, Oxon OX14 4RN

and by Routledge
605 Third Avenue, New York, NY 10158

Routledge is an imprint of the Taylor & Francis Group, an informa business

British Library Cataloguing-in-Publication Data
A catalogue record for this book is available from the British Library

Library of Congress Cataloging-in-Publication Data
A catalog record has been requested for this book

ISBN: 978-0-367-33059-0 (hbk)
ISBN: 978-0-367-33058-3 (pbk)
ISBN: 978-0-429-31779-8 (ebk)

DOI: 10.4324/9780429317798

Typeset in Bembo
by Newgen Publishing UK

CONTENTS

ACKNOWLEDGEMENTS

We would like to gratefully acknowledge the kind assistance of Prof. Sue Starfield and Dr. James Corcoran, both of whom read and gave feedback on an earlier version of the manuscript for this book. As authors, we, of course, are responsible for any remaining errors or infelicities in this final version.

1

INTRODUCTION

The field of *English for Research Publication Purposes* (ERPP) has developed in response to the rise of English as the global lingua franca of scientific research and publication and the need of international researchers to publish in English. The term *English for Research Publication Purposes* and its ERPP acronym were first used, to our knowledge, by Sally Burgess and Margaret Cargill in a special edition of the *Journal of English for Academic Purposes* in 2008 (Cargill & Burgess, 2008, p. 75). In the introduction to that volume, they provide a definition of the field as follows:

> English for Research Publication Purposes (ERPP) can be thought of as a branch of EAP [English for Academic Purposes] addressing the concerns of professional researchers and post-graduate students who need to publish in peer-reviewed international journals.
>
> (parentheses added)

The special edition brought together papers which had previously been presented at the first PRISEAL conference (*Publishing and Presenting Research Internationally: Issues for Speakers of English as an Additional Language*) in Tenerife, Spain in 2007. It is this conference and the ensuing special edition which really put ERPP on the map and since then the field has grown exponentially. Another important landmark and a result of the exponential growth in interest in ERPP was the establishment in 2020 of its own dedicated international refereed journal, *Journal of Research Publication Purposes* (JERPP), co-edited (with Sue Starfield) by one of the authors of this book, Pejman Habibie.

Leading up to these landmarks, there had been a growing realisation that many scholars who used English as an additional language (EAL) had difficulty in participating in the international world of research because of linguistic difficulties or other non-discursive (Canagarajah, 1996) reasons related to being located outside

DOI: 10.4324/9780429317798-1

the main centres of knowledge production. Thus, while the initial impetus for ERPP, as indicated in the sub-title of the PRISEAL conference (*Issues for Speakers of English as an Additional Language*), was to help scholars whose first language was not English, the field has expanded to take in all professional researchers and post-graduate students, that is, Anglophone as well as EAL scholars; this is because it was realised that all scholars may be in need of help in navigating the intricacies of the research and publication "game" (Casanave, 2002). This broader conception not-withstanding, it is the case that most ERPP research to date has been focused on scholars whose first language is not English. ERPP is thus a specialised approach to English language and literacy education focused on all those writing for research publication, whether they be scholars for whom English is an additional language or Anglophone scholars.

The above developments have meant that ERPP is now an established field of study. In spite of a considerable literature and a dedicated journal, however, there is to date no single book that gathers this work together and tries to make sense of it in an all-embracing and coherent manner. The goal of this volume is therefore to fill this gap and provide a comprehensive overview of what ERPP encompasses as a scholarly field, including its antecedents, its disciplinary boundaries, its competing discourses, and its principal research and practice paradigms. In this introductory overview, we do not intend to present a particular position, but to provide a neutral, balanced, but at the same time critical view. Indeed, as authors, we come from rather different scholarly trajectories, with one of us (Flowerdew) having devoted many years to studying the research and publication activities of plurilingual scholars in Hong Kong and Mainland China and the other (Habibie) having more recently entered the field with a focus on the writing for publication struggles of Anglophone scholars in Canada. The research and theoretical dimensions of the book, we hope, will be of interest to both novice and established researchers in applied linguistics and TESOL in general, and English for Academic Purposes, academic writing, writing studies, and second language writing, in particular. The pedagogical aspect, we hope, will appeal to graduate students, faculty supervisors, doctoral advisors, ESP/EAP/ERPP practitioners, and EAP curriculum and material designers and developers. The book also has implications for those teaching professional academic writing skills, journal editors and reviewers, and authors' editors.

The scope of ERPP

ERPP constitutes an academic field concerned with the investigation of the nature and use of English in research and publication contexts and at the same time a field of practice focused on the needs of those who wish to publish in international journals. As such, both tendencies are informed by theory – social theories, theories of discourse, theories of communication, and theories of teaching and learning. In terms of research methods, ERPP employs both quantitative and qualitative methods, including survey (both questionnaire and in-depth interview); natural-istic case study (single or multiple); genre analysis (including corpus-based genre analysis); content analysis; and political and philosophical analysis. It is not noted for experimental research, although, as an eclectic field, it is open to any method. While some research is focused on more theoretical considerations, other work is more directly concerned with the practical constraints of teaching and learning. With many ERPP publications, however, research and pedagogy go hand in hand. Most ERPP research can be described as problem-driven, seeking as it does to address the concerns of professional scholars and postgraduate students, as in Burgess and Cargill's definition above, but in a research-informed manner.

A great deal of ERPP research has been conducted following one of two broad theoretical approaches: genre analysis (a branch of discourse analysis which studies "communicative events which are associated with particular settings and which have recognised structures and communicative functions" [Flowerdew, 2002, p. 183]) and social constructivism (a theory that views learning as primarily taking place in social and cultural settings rather than solely within the individual [Fry, Kettering, & Marshall, 2008]). Although genre analysis takes account of the communicative setting and the community of participants who use a given genre (its discourse community, [Swales, 1990]), the analysis tends to be focused on the product of the communicative event, the text (spoken or written). The goal of this approach to ERPP is to provide descriptions of academic genres which can help better understand how knowledge is communicated and to feed into ERPP pedagogy. Most of this work is concerned with research articles (RAs), but other ERPP-related academic genres have been analysed, including some occluded genres (genres not in the public domain), such as referees' reports, editors' letters, and research grant proposals. The main ERPP-related genres in the public domain are RAs, book reviews, conference presentations, and academic blogs. The genre analytic approach to ERPP research is the older of the two, predating the social constructivist tendency, in fact, because there has been an interest in scientific text for many decades (Barber, 1962; Halliday, 2004; Huddleston, 1971; Selinker, Tarone, & Hanzeli, 1981; Tarone, Dwyer, Gillette, & Icke, 1998), although much of this early work did not take context much into account.

The social constructivist approach to ERPP research views text production as a social practice, investigating such issues as scholars' writing procedures, their interactions with colleagues and gatekeepers (editors and referees), and the pressures brought to bear on them in their various contexts (Canagarajah, 1996, 2002; Flowerdew, 2001; Li, 2006a, 2006b, 2007a, 2007b, 2014a, 2014b; Lillis & Curry, 2010; Mu, 2020). The goal of this approach is to develop an understanding of the modus operandi and practical experiences in going about writing for publication of distinct groups of writers and individuals. Situated accounts of scholars' practices and of their perceptions, problems, and strategies concerning such practices can serve as exemplars against which other situations can be compared. They may also serve to bring about policy changes at either a local or broader level, and they may feed into pedagogy. The earliest study using the social constructivist approach is St John's (1987) investigation into the composing processes of 30 Spanish scientists writing for publication in English at the University of Córdoba, Spain. St John conducted her investigation because she wanted to find out how her university in the United Kingdom (Aston University) could better design courses to assist her target group of EAL writers. More than this, though, her study provided a baseline against which future researchers and practitioners could measure their own results and practices, respectively.

Given that an important goal of both approaches just outlined is pedagogic, ERPP pedagogy, that is to say, how to teach ERPP, can be considered an important third strand (Li & Flowerdew, 2020; Li, Flowerdew, & Cargill, 2018). Indeed, many practitioners would see this as the most important of the three. In order to be able to provide appropriate pedagogy, a teacher of ERPP requires a deep understanding of the rhetorical practices of the discourse communities the scholars they teach are coming from. In order to arrive at such an understanding, they need the necessary tools to do so. This is hopefully where this book comes in, by establishing a link between the research base of ERPP and the field of ERPP practice – learning how to teach research English.

There are also other research domains interacting with ERPP, including philosophy and history of science (Atkinson, 1999; Bazerman, 1988; Latour & Woolgar, 1986), policy studies relating to research and publication (Feng, Beckett, & Huang, 2013; Lee & Lee, 2013); issues of linguistic policy and (in)justice (Ammon, 2000; Pronskikh, 2018); language, or domain, loss (Bennett, 2007; Bordet, 2016); World Englishes and English as a Lingua Franca (Flowerdew, 2015); predatory journals (Soler & Cooper, 2017); and many others. In the next section, we will provide an overview of the rest of the book.

Overview of the book

In Chapter 2, *The background to ERPP*, we map out the growing pressure to publish that scholars are facing, commonly referred to as publish or perish, and the exponential rise in international English-medium academic journals and the number of international scholars seeking to publish in those journals. We set the scene by unpacking the global socio-political and socio-economic factors that have contributed to the current situation. We deal with key systems such as globalisation and neoliberalism and how they have resulted in the expansion and internationalisation of higher education and the importance and implications of those concepts for ERPP. Massification of higher education and marketisation of universities are also topics discussed in this chapter. The discussion elaborates on how such phenomena shape the globalisation of scholarship and consequently scholarly publication in English-medium academic journals. Finally, given that EAL scholars are in the majority worldwide, we briefly discuss how scholarly publication in English linguistically disadvantages such scholars and poses challenges to their visibility and participation in global scholarship.

In Chapter 3, *From the Scientific Enlightenment to publish or perish*, we begin with a historical perspective and look at the emergence of modern empirical science and scientific inquiry during the 17th century Enlightenment, along with the development of academic communication and scholarly exchange since this period. Then, we focus on the RA and explore its emergence and development as the most prestigious scholarly genre in academic discourse. We briefly analyse its rhetorical structure and contours, constituent components and sections, and linguistic properties and features. Again, tracing its history back to the Enlightenment, we discuss the development of the peer-review mechanism as an essential feature of publish or perish, along with the more recent assessment and quantification tools of impact factor, and h-index. We also discuss the issue of authorship assignment and publication output expectations, as these can also affect scholarly performance measurement.

Chapter 4, *Discourses and perspectives on English*, focuses on various conceptual approaches to the English language and their relevance to ERPP. The chapter contrasts two particular perspectives on English as a Global Language: *laissez-faire* liberalism and linguistic imperialism (Pennycook, 2000). The first of these approaches sees English as a beneficial, global lingua franca which allows for equal communication between countries and regions, while the second emphasises the socio-political, economic, and cultural agendas of Global English and its extensive and growing hegemonic power. We address the question as to whether there is a middle way between these two highly contrastive discourses on English. Next, we address the issue of *domain loss*, the loss of language use in certain domains and genres due to them being overtaken by English. We sketch out the ramifications of this concept with regard to ERPP and global knowledge production. With the rise of English as the dominant language of research and publication and the fact that most scholars now use English as an additional language, a question of equity arises. A lot of research in ERPP has addressed this issue and this research is mapped out. More recently, a counter-discourse has developed arguing that all scholars have to deal with the challenges of writing for publication and that more attention should be given to Anglophones. This more recent literature is also summarised. The chapter finally highlights World Englishes (the varieties of English as it is used in different contexts around the world) and English as a Lingua Franca (English as a global means of communication between communities) as conceptions of English which impinge on approaches to ERPP.

Chapter 5, *Theoretical orientations in ERPP*, focuses on theories and approaches that have been drawn upon or developed in the context of ERPP. The theories covered are genre theory, social constructivist theory, and World Systems Theory. Genre theory has been very important in ERPP because it provides a predictive and analytical lens to explore discursive and generic challenges and problems that peripheral scholars or novice and doctoral researchers encounter in their writing. Additionally, systematic descriptions of the distinguishing features of genres provide teaching goals for ERPP pedagogy. Two related approaches within the overall paradigm of social constructivism are considered: academic literacies and situated learning. Academic literacies is an approach to literacy which considers reading and writing as social practices. This means that reading and writing need to be studied in their context of use. Much ERPP research has taken this approach and used interview and other ethnographic methods to find out how people go about writing in their academic communities. The situated learning approach takes an apprenticeship perspective and considers learning to write for publication as a form of apprenticeship situated in an academic community. It is a powerful model which can interpret how novice scholars develop into professionals. Some important notions with regard to social constructivist theories are identity, power, and agency, and these are reviewed, along with various ERPP studies which draw upon these concepts.

The concepts of core and (semi)periphery countries and regions are presented as the key notions within World Systems theory (Wallerstein, 1974). These concepts have been borrowed from economics and politics to understand the knowledge economy at a global level and the positions and role of different countries and regions in the production and dissemination of scholarship. ERPP research has shown how access to international publication is more difficult from the periphery and semi-periphery countries and regions, most of which have restricted economic and educational resources, on the one hand, and do not have English as their first language, on the other.

In Chapter 6, *Research approaches in ERPP*, we take a closer look at two approaches to research which have been very fruitful for ERPP studies: genre analysis and naturalistic approaches. We examined the theoretical perspectives of these two approaches in Chapter 5, but here we focus on the empirical work that has been conducted within the framework of these two theories. Genre analysis, as a branch of discourse analysis, has a relatively long history in mainstream English for Academic Purposes research, but a lot of this work, in examining the discourses of scholarly publication (in particular the RA, but also other scholarly genres), is very valuable for ERPP. Such an approach has helped to develop an in-depth understanding of discipline-specific rhetorical structures and formal features of scholarly genres. This knowledge then can be useful in developing pedagogical interventions and materials needed for ERPP education. We review a considerable amount of this work.

Unlike text-oriented genre analytic approaches, naturalistic approaches are embedded in the academic literacies and situated learning paradigms and are ethnographically oriented in terms of methodology. In these approaches, writing for scholarly publication is considered as a social practice that is shaped and informed by surrounding socio-contextual discourses and practices and ideological and political forces. After setting out the tenets of this approach, we review a number of studies which have been insightful in teaching us how scholars actually go about writing for publication in various contexts and the networks that are involved in this enterprise. Just as genre analysis can feed into teaching writing for publication, so too can the more ethnographic accounts created by the naturalistic approaches, in revealing how scholars go about writing and negotiating publication (Paltridge, Starfield, & Tardy, 2016).

Chapter 7, *Gatekeeping and peer review*, addresses the publication review process as a gatekeeping mechanism in the production and dissemination of knowledge and focuses on a strand of research within ERPP that has looked at editors and reviewers as one of the key stakeholders in scholarly publication. More specifically, the chapter surveys some of the scholarship that has explored the views and perspectives of editors and reviewers regarding effective writing and publishing. It explores the literature that has examined the characteristics of competent reviewers and good review reports and some of the research that has investigated the experiences of editors and reviewers in the gatekeeping process and their perspectives on their responsibilities. The chapter also deals with the controversial topic of editorial bias, presenting contradictory narratives regarding the existence or non-existence of systematic bias in scholarly publication, especially towards EAL scholars (Hyland, 2016, 2020). Finally, the chapter reviews studies that have analysed the discourse of peer review and the discursive interactions between editors, reviewers, and authors, identifying some of the discursive and linguistic characteristics of the occluded genres of peer-review reports and editors' letters.

Focusing on the advancement of technology and the emergence of digital tools, in Chapter 8, *ERPP and the digital age*, we deal with the topic of digitalisation of scholarly publication and its implications for the construction and dissemination of knowledge. More specifically, we discuss how different technologies have changed and sometimes revolutionised the landscape of academic publication in recent years. We classify these changes under four overarching frameworks: ethnoscape, epistemoscape, genrescape, and pedigoscape. Accordingly, ethnoscape frames the ways in which new technologies have changed and reconfigured the socialisation and interactions within and beyond academic territories, disciplines, and communities. It shows how digitalisation has blurred the spatio-temporal boundaries separating traditional academic discourse communities. Epistemoscape addresses the impact of digital technologies, especially the worldwide web, on the global knowledge economy and the possibilities afforded by those technologies in terms of access to, distribution, and management of knowledge and scholarship. Genrescape deals with how digitalisation has spurred the emergence of new genres for the production and distribution of scholarship. It explains how digital platforms provide unprecedented opportunities for multimodal collaborative knowledge construction, publication, and adjudication that go way beyond traditional textual practices. Finally, the pedigoscape deals with the implications of digitalisation for ERPP teaching and learning. It elaborates on how digital technologies can help academics, especially novice scholars, to gain insights into the inner workings of the publication system and how such technological tools can scaffold their socialisation into the academic publication process.

Chapter 9, *ERPP pedagogy*, as is clear from the title, is focused on the teaching and learning of ERPP. Working with the premise that there can be no one single model, the chapter reviews various modes of delivery and pedagogical approaches to ERPP. Using Kwan's (2010) competencies taxonomy as the point of departure, we present a pedagogical framework that can be applied in ERPP courses and can help develop the required literacies for writing for scholarly publication. Next, we review some of the modes of teaching and learning that are available for ERPP.

They include supervisory mentorship; how-to manuals; course books; courses and workshops; and writing groups and retreats. We then move on to methodological approaches, discussing task- and genre-based pedagogy; corpus-based approaches; and critical-pragmatic approaches. We highlight the key features of each of these approaches (which are not by any means mutually exclusive). We conclude the chapter by pointing out that teacher education for ERPP is a sorely neglected area.

In the final chapter, Chapter 10, *Conclusion*, we begin by noting that ERPP as a field of research and practice has come a long way in the last 25 years or so. We sketch out some of the areas we have not had time or space to deal with in enough detail in the main body of the book and highlight some of the areas and issues that are ripe for further ERPP scholarship. We consider the place of ERPP in the university of today, both in terms of policy and practice. Finally, we speculate on the future of ERPP and English as the language of international research and publication.

2
THE BACKGROUND TO ERPP

Introduction: Publish or perish

Publish or perish is an expression which refers to the need of academics to have a good publication record in order not to jeopardise their careers (Li, 2014a; Rawat & Meena, 2014), although it has now extended to also include students studying for their doctorate, or even their Master's degree (Flowerdew, 2013a). In recent decades, there has been an exponential growth in the number of researchers, academic journals, and scholarly research articles (RAs) published internationally. The publish or perish culture has been spreading to all corners of the globe. According to a report produced in 2018 for the International Association of Scientific, Technical and Medical Publishers (Johnson, Watkinson, & Mabe, 2018), in that year, there were about 33,100 active scholarly peer-reviewed English-language journals, publishing over three million articles a year. The number of researchers in 2018 stood between seven and eight million, depending on definition (p. 25). While the United States (US) has until recently been considered to be the driving force behind international research and publication, China has now overtaken that country to become the most important investor in scientific research and producer of research papers globally (Johnson, Watkinson, & Mabe, 2018). In 2018, China produced 19% of global RAs and the US 18%, with India, also increasing rapidly in recent years, at 5%, just above Germany, the United Kingdom (UK), and Japan, each on 4% (Johnson, Watkinson, & Mabe, 2018). These numbers and trends are likely to have only increased by the time this book goes to press.

The term publish or perish was first coined nearly a hundred years ago (Coolidge, 1932, p. 308), but it has become a lot more relevant today. Certainly, a good publication record reflects well on a scholar and can enhance the reputation of their academic department and university, as well as help them with their personal career aspirations. Often forgotten, research and publication can bring personal satisfaction

DOI: 10.4324/9780429317798-2

to an individual scholar. The quest for knowledge and its dissemination is, after all, along with a desire to teach and pass on knowledge to students, a primary motivation for embarking on an academic career in the first place. In the past, when there was less emphasis on publication, many scholars did excellent work which was never disseminated. Many a PhD thesis, in particular, has mouldered in a university library basement, never to be read or cited. In today's research and publication world, however, PhD work is much more likely to be published. With electronic publishing nowadays, publication is much quicker and research findings can be disseminated very rapidly.

From the university's and the academic department's point of view, also, publication record can be an effective and objective measure of achievement when it comes to hiring, contract renewal, tenure, or promotion of the individual concerned. Furthermore, universities can use the reputations of their academic staff to promote the university in the eyes of sponsors (government or private) and prospective students or academic staff. On the other side of the coin, however, the "perish" side, academic staff who do not have a strong track record in publication may be sanctioned – in terms of non-renewal of contract, failure to achieve promotion, or imposition of a heavier teaching load – even though they may be excellent teachers and/or administrators.

There is, in fact, a range of negative effects which may arise from overdue pressure to publish. To take some examples in random order. First, disciplinary variation may mean that scholars working in niche fields of study are at a disadvantage, because their research is likely to be read by fewer people and consequently less likely to be cited. Second, research in some fields may take much longer to carry out and consequently result in fewer publications than in others. Third, there may be a temptation to publish more average or below average papers rather than fewer above average ones: a case of quantity taking precedence over quality. Fourth, publication pressure may lead to academics neglecting their teaching and other responsibilities. Fifth, there may be a temptation to engage in unethical practices, such as "salami-slicing" (the slicing up of research into a number of publications instead of one), plagiarism (copying ideas or language from other authors), and self-plagiarism (repeating oneself in more than one publication). Sixth, pressure to publish has also led to the proliferation of so-called predatory journals (Beall, 2010), journals which offer publication without the normal quality assurance measures or practices, but which charge a fee and prey on young, inexperienced scholars and scholars desperate for publications, in particular (Kolata, 2017; Sudhira, 2018). Seventh, international publication is becoming more and more often a requirement of doctoral or even Master's degree graduation (Flowerdew, 2013a), putting extra pressure on graduate students.

All of these contentious issues (and others) merit further investigation and fall within the scope of ERPP. Looked at in a more positive light, however, publish or perish does have the effect of motivating scholars to conduct research and produce publications. In the greater scheme of things, it creates knowledge and benefits society. In the rest of this chapter, we will consider the confluence of factors which have given rise to the additional impetus to publish or perish and ultimately to the need for the academic field of ERPP. These factors are:

- globalisation and neoliberalism;
- English as the global lingua franca;
- English and the globalisation of scholarship;
- the massification of tertiary education;
- universities as engines of economic growth and national prestige;
- the marketisation of universities.

Globalisation and neoliberalism

Globalisation and neoliberalism are important concepts for ERPP, because they underpin the expansion and internationalisation of university education, the rise of English as the international lingua franca of research and publication, and the global increase in the culture of publish or perish.

Globalisation is the process by which human relations at all levels are expanded across national borders, be that by trade, the movement of people, or cross-border (electronic) communication (Giddens, 1990; Robertson, 1992). It is a process that has been going on for centuries, but it intensified during the 1980s and 1990s, as a result of the development of information technology, mass immigration, cheap travel, and the development of English as an international lingua franca, among other factors (Giddens, 1990; Robertson, 1992). One of the results of globalisation is that universities have become much more international and that teachers and students have become much more internationally mobile.

Neoliberalism is related to globalisation. It is an economic and political theory which holds that free trade, free markets, deregulation (a decrease in government control and regulation), and the privatisation of state-run monopolies are for the greater good (Harvey, 2005). Some would say that neoliberalism is driven by globalisation insofar as it depends on international flows of capital and people. According to the neoliberal philosophy, it is consumers who determine the direction that economies take, not governments. "Choice", "competition", and the "free market" are three of its main tenets. Although there are many criticisms of neoliberalism, including its tendency to endanger workers' rights and the sovereign rights of nations, it is the predominant economic force globally in the current era and determines how economies function (Harvey, 2005). It is important for ERPP, as it underpins the way contemporary universities are run.

English as the global lingua franca

Over the centuries, English has developed from being the national language of a few million people living in parts of what was later to become the United Kingdom to being a global lingua spoken and written in all parts of the globe (Crystal, 2003). Today, there are somewhere between 350 and 400 million native speakers of English spread across different countries that have adopted English as their first language, but there are also some 900 million people in other countries who are familiar with English as an additional language (EAL) (Eberhard, Simons, & Fennig, 2020). Given a world population of about 7.8 billion, this means that between approximately 4.5% and 5% of the world's population have English as their first language, about 11.5% have English as an additional language, and about 16.5% have English as either their first or an additional language. These are very rough estimates and they do not tell us anything about the proficiency level of those who know English as an additional language. Nevertheless, they do tell us two important things: first, that English is widely spoken across the world, and second that Anglophones are very much outnumbered by those who have English as an additional language.

In terms of the motivation of those who have learned or are learning English as an additional language, some may do so for the traditional reasons for learning a foreign language: its cognitive benefits and cultural enrichment. Nowadays, however, the attraction of learning English is more often much more pragmatic. English is now learned because it is the most important language for international communication, the internet, international business, international entertainment, and, most important for this book, international education, scientific research, and publication (Crystal, 2003). As an aside, although there are folk beliefs that English is an easy language to learn (it has a simple grammar, etc.), that it is clear and concise, and that is why it has been adopted as the language of research and publication (see e.g., Englander & Corcoran, 2019), there is no scientific evidence to show that any one language is intrinsically easier than other languages. The apparent difficulty of a language depends upon how close the language is to one's first language (Bowerman & Levinson, 2001). While a speaker of Dutch or German may not find English particularly difficult, it certainly represents more of a challenge for speakers of non-Indo-European languages, such as Chinese, Japanese, Arabic, or Russian.

Rather than any supposed easiness of learning, the rise of English is due to a coming together of a number of socio-economic factors (Englander, 2014). The initial impetus for the spread of the English language was British colonisation (Pennycook, 1994; Phillipson, 1992, 2009). However, since the First World War, the United Kingdom has declined as an international power and dominance has passed to the US, which has greater economic, technological, and media influence (Crystal, 2003).

English and the globalisation of scholarship

Of particular relevance for this book is the leading position that the US took in research and development through its world-leading universities. Until recently, the US has been the country with the highest academic publications output by far and this is one of the important reasons for the role of English as the lingua franca of scientific research and publication. While German and French were important international languages of publication up until the Second World War, the research cultures of France and Germany were crippled as a result of the conflict and the US was the only country to come out of the war with its educational and research infrastructure undamaged (Ammon, 2001). This meant more publication in English and less in French and German. Furthermore, research and publication were supported in the US by huge investment in research and development during the Cold War of the 1950s, 60s, and 70s (Ammon, 2001). As a result of these developments, North American researchers set the language, theories, models, and standards which have become the accepted norms (and some would say therefore have an unfair advantage) (Aïssaoui, Geringer, & Livanis, 2021; Bajwa & Konig, 2019; Üsdiken, 2014). Although China has now overtaken the US in terms of scholarly output (Johnson, Watkinson, & Mabe, 2018), it seems that Chinese universities and researchers are content (at least for the time being) to use English as their language of publication, because it provides access to knowledge, on the one hand, and a global audience for their own research, on the other.

A common language facilitates the global exchange of information (Ammon, 2001; Lillis & Curry, 2010; Swales, 2004). This is why increasing numbers of journals are publishing in English and why scholars internationally, whether they have English as their first language or not, are seeking to disseminate their findings in English. This is the best way to bring their research to the attention of the scientific community, which has increasingly become international. We might add that this pressure to disseminate research findings in English is the most obvious reason for the growth of interest in ERPP. As evidence of this preponderance of English, the best-known database to cover research and publication across the disciplines is the *Web of Science*, currently curated by Clarivate Analytics,[1] (previously a branch of the Canadian company Thomson Reuters). It tracks the number of citations accruing to journals. The published selection process for inclusion of journals in this database is as follows:

> English is the universal language of science at this time in history. It is for this reason that Thomson Scientific focuses on journals that publish full text in English or at very least, their bibliographic information in English. There are many journals covered in Web of Science that publish only their bibliographic information in English with full text in another language. However, going forward, it is clear that the journals most important to the international research community will publish full text in English.
>
> *Clarivate Analytics, 2020*

Also contributing to the preponderance of English in research, or perhaps as a result of it (it is a reflexive relationship), universities are increasingly introducing English as the medium of instruction. In the European Union, this process has been promoted through the Erasmus exchange programme, established to promote student mobility within the European Union, but since extended through Erasmus+ and Erasmus Mundus to other countries (Erasmus+, 2021). These programmes have increased the demand for (academic) English-language proficiency. Similar international student exchange programmes are offered by other countries. Furthermore, research is increasingly conducted internationally, by teams of researchers, (Chinchilla-Rodriguez et al., 2018; Lillis & Curry, 2010; Ribeiro, Rapini, Alves Silva, & Alburquerque, 2018), with access to Anglophone collaborators an important factor in the make-up of these teams (Aïssaoui, Geringer, & Livanis, 2021).

In spite of this emphasis on English, there are still many regional or national journals, usually published in national languages (although even here there is a move towards English) (Salager-Meyer, 2008, 2014, 2015). In 2018, Johnson, Watkinson, and Mabe (2018) estimated there to be 9,400 peer-reviewed non-English-language journals published by the International Association of Scientific, Technical and Medical Publishers (compared to, as noted above, 33,100 peer-reviewed English-language journals). The non-English, regional or national journals tend to focus on applied research or social matters of particular relevance to the local community (Flowerdew & Li, 2009; López-Navarro, Moreno, Quintanilla, & Rey-Rocha, 2015). Scholars tend to publish in these journals as a service to the local community and through a desire to communicate with their linguistic peers (or, surprisingly not emphasised in the literature, because they do not have the requisite skills to write and publish in English) (Flowerdew & Li, 2009). More universally relevant research tends to be published in international journals (which publish in English), where scholars can receive wider recognition (López-Navarro et al., 2015), not only from their international peers, but also from their universities and national assessment bodies, which attach more value to international journals publishing in English (Lillis, 2012; Sheridan, 2015). This research published in English also tends to be what scholars consider to be their "best" research. As Salager-Meyer (2015) puts it, "[scholars on the periphery] prefer to submit their best papers (i.e., the most original, ground-breaking and/or scientifically robust ones) to English-written journals with a high impact factor [i.e., frequently cited]" (p. 21). This tendency has been noted in studies by Flowerdew and Li (2009) in Hong Kong; by Li and Flowerdew (2009) in mainland China; by Duszak and Lewkowicz (2008) in Poland; and by López-Navarro et al. (2015) in Spain, among others. These studies have also noted that there is less focus on local journals from natural sciences disciplines, where concerns tend to be more universal, and more focus from humanities and social science disciplines, where local and applied issues are more prominent.

We would be remiss if we did not mention some of the negative aspects of English as a global lingua franca of scholarship (Ammon, 2016; Corcoran, 2019; Flowerdew, 2013a). For example, scholars who are not able to publish in English are excluded from the global conversation. This may not only be considered to be unfair on them, but also is a loss to the global community. Gibbs (1995) has referred to this phenomenon as "lost science". Conversely, EAL scholars who publish only in English may be depriving their national and/or regional communities of important research results which may be of value to local professionals and decision makers (Di Bitetti & Ferreras, 2017). We will consider the more critical views of English in the following chapters.

Massification of tertiary education

Participation in tertiary education has been growing exponentially for the last several decades, a process referred to as *massification* (Usher, 2017). In 1900, only 1% of people attended university. A century later, this number had increased two-hundredfold to 20%, with rates in some industrialised countries climbing past 50% and even 80% (Schofer & Meyer, 2005, p. 898). A great amount of this increase in the latter part of the 20th century has been in Asia, China in particular, but growth has also been evident in Latin America, Africa, and North America. There has been a relatively less rapid increase in Western Europe, due to demographic factors, albeit that this latter trend has been mitigated by increases in international students, especially in the UK, but also in other European countries (Usher, 2017). The massification of university education worldwide has been made possible by increases in national gross domestic product (GDP) in many countries, particularly, again, in Asia. This economic growth has allowed governments to invest in greater tertiary education provision and allowed individuals in those countries to have the option of travelling abroad to study, if they so wish (and have the necessary financial resources).

If the numbers of students have risen exponentially, then so too has the number of university teachers required to teach all of these students. University teachers, if they want to build a career, are more and more often required to pursue research and publish their findings. Greater numbers of scholars seeking publication makes it more difficult to publish in the top journals, putting extensive pressure on researchers. As a result of this, more journals have been started and this has created further opportunities for researchers to publish. The process is thus a self-fulfilling one: increases in student numbers mean increases in the numbers of scholars; increases in the numbers of scholars mean more manuscripts seeking a home; more manuscripts seeking a home mean more journals are created; which in turn encourages more manuscripts, and the process starts again.

Universities as engines of economic growth and national prestige

Universities are seen by governments as engines of economic growth (Valero & Van Reenen, 2016). Human capital is essential for economic progress and scientific research can lead to technological innovation. In addition, universities are, in theory, good for social mobility, which in turn promotes economic growth. At a regional level, furthermore, if a university is created in a town or city, it will attract a relatively affluent population who will be purchasers of goods and services. This translates to the national and international levels. Nations promote their universities internationally, because they want to attract foreign students, who will add to the GDP of the nation. The following quotation from an article in the *Financial Times* (Jack, 2017, par. 1) is indicative of this trend:

> Government targets sharp growth in foreign student numbers. ... The British government is seeking to increase the number of international students attending higher education in the UK by nearly a third to 600,000 in the coming decade, according to an education strategy unveiled on Saturday ... The objective to raise foreign student numbers from 460,000 today is part of efforts to significantly boost annual education exports from £20bn to £35bn by 2030.

The Anglophone countries (the US, the UK, and Australia, in particular) are especially successful in this sphere, attracting hundreds of thousands of overseas students, who, incidentally, are willing to pay high fees (which can pay for research and publication). But other non-Anglophone countries are also active in this area, offering degree programmes in English to allow for what would otherwise be a language barrier. In order to attract international students, countries as diverse as France, Germany, the Netherlands, and China – countries which have no traditional link to the English language – offer programmes of study in the medium of English.

Top-class universities are also a symbol of national prestige. National governments want to be able to say that they have excellent universities, not only to attract international students and boost the national budget, but also as an instrument of "soft power", as an indication that they are an advanced country on a par with the best in the world. In Russia, for example, in order to boost five Russian universities into the international top 100, financial incentives have been given to a selected number of institutions (O'Malley, 2016). China has taken similar measures to promote its leading universities internationally. It has also offered very generous salaries and conditions of service to attract Chinese scholars working overseas back to the country in order to boost its universities. As another example, there is no doubt that the prestige of British universities was enhanced when, in 2020, two of their universities, Oxford and University College, London, were taking the lead in the development of a COVID-19 vaccine. The presence of top-class universities in the UK has been trumpeted by the government of the country in order to help persuade the public that the UK can "go it alone" after Brexit (exiting from the European Union). Here is another quotation from the *Financial Times*, cited earlier (Jack, 2017, par. 6):

> Damian Hinds, education secretary, said: "The UK's education system is world-leading and its reputation is the envy of many countries around the globe. As we prepare to leave the EU it is more important than ever to reach out to our global partners and maximise the potential of our best assets — that includes our education offer and the international students this attracts."

Marketisation of universities

The marketisation of universities refers to the process by which universities have transformed themselves from being elite centres of scholarship and learning to consumer-oriented corporate entities responding to the forces of supply and demand and the profit motive (Brown, 2011). Although throughout history all universities have been under some sort of government or religious control, in many cases, they have traditionally had a high degree of autonomy and managed themselves on democratic lines through senates or similar decision-making bodies. Their policies have been guided by two basic principles: first, creation of knowledge for its own sake and for the greater good of humanity, and second, dissemination of this knowledge to their students, again for the good of society (Gerber, 2014). Universities have historically tended to resist over-expansion and have not been motivated by profit (Gerber, 2014).

However, modern "marketised" universities operate more like business corporations. They are most prevalent in the US and the UK, the pioneers of neo-liberalism. China is also rapidly adopting this model. The universities in continental Europe, on the other hand, have been slower in this respect, although they are moving in that direction. While the professoriate still has a say in academic matters in the marketised universities, they are led by more business-oriented managers. These managers will seek to maximise income through student fees, expansion of the numbers of students they can cater for, and government and private sector research funding. Concomitant with the expansionist policies of these marketised universities is the need to employ more academics, who will likely be required to publish. Graduate students are also likely to need to publish, putting further pressure on the system. In passing, we might comment that, unfortunately, many of these market-oriented universities have borrowed large sums of money and become very reliant on fees from international students. They have as a result been put in a precarious position because of the COVID-19 pandemic (Drayton & Waltmann, 2020; Thatcher, Zhang, Todoroski, Chau, Wang, & Liang, 2020).

As a promotional tool, market-oriented universities make use of university league tables to sell themselves. University league tables, or rankings, are a way of measuring university performance on a number of objective and more qualitative measures, including staff/student ratios; average number of publications and citations per academic staff member; research funding; percentage of international students; and peer-ranking (by scholars in other universities). The best-known ranking systems are *QS World University Rankings* and *Shanghai Jiao Tong University Ranking*. University rankings are very powerful in a number of ways. Prospective students may consider the ranking of a university when deciding where to study; universities can use their ranking as a way to attract government and private funding for research, development, and endowments; top-class scholars are likely to choose to work in high-ranking universities; and governments can use rankings as a means of controlling universities, by rewarding universities for good performance in the tables and sanctioning their lesser-performing counterparts.

Publish or perish is not equally spread

Having enumerated a range of factors leading to publish or perish in the previous sections, it is important to point out that this phenomenon is not equally spread across individual institutions, university systems, nations, or regions (Üsdiken, 2014). At the international and regional level, World Systems Theory (Wallerstein, 1974, 2004) posits that the world can be divided into the rich developed countries (the centre) and the poorer less-developed countries (the periphery). This dichotomy can be applied to university systems and publication regimes (see Chapter 4), where periphery countries have fewer resources to participate in international knowledge creation. Lower adoption of the publish or perish model has been linked to a range of factors. Economic resource constraints may limit access to expensive databases, opportunities for networking and conference participation, and English-language skills training. Cultural constraints include greater importance attached to non-English publications, greater prestige attached to different publication formats (e.g., books rather than indexed articles), and less emphasis put on the North American positivist research paradigm. A further factor affecting participation in publish or perish is levels of international collaboration and mobility (see Aïssaoui, Geringer, & Livanis [2021] for review of all these factors). At the country level, Geertz (1983) alluded a long time ago to the centre/periphery nature of the research capacity in the university system within the US (also, more recently Swales, 2019), and similar institutional hierarchies exist in all countries. Nevertheless, in spite of this variability, it is important to emphasise that the drift is very much towards publish or perish, on both a global and a national level, and not away from it.

English as an additional language for most international scholars

One of the results of the increasing use of English as the international language of research and publication is that, as referred to above, more and more scholars who do not have English as their mother tongue need to publish in English. In fact, probably the majority of scholars publishing in English internationally are having to write in a language which is not their mother tongue. Scholars in the field of ERPP refer to such writers as EAL (English as an additional language) writers. This designation is often preferred to the commonly used "non-native speaker" (or "writer" in the case of ERPP), because the "non-" descriptor in the latter term suggests that something is missing and the term is thus discriminatory (Holliday, 2005). The term EAL writer acknowledges that such writers are already competent writers and/or speakers of at least one native language. The term second language writer (L2 writer) is also used as a synonym of EAL writer, although, again, some scholars avoid using this acronym (Curry & Lillis, 2013).

The relationship between L1 and EAL/L2 writers is not a binary distinction. EAL writers may be as equally proficient in English as their Anglophone counterparts, or even better. They may have worked hard over a long period of time to match up to the L1 standard, or they may have benefitted from schooling in English, be that at nursery, primary, secondary, or tertiary level. Increasingly, education is being offered through the medium of English in many countries where it is not the official language. In countries where English is a second language (ESL), as opposed to a foreign language (EFL), English may be the preferred language for certain functions, especially written genres. In those countries, universities may use English as the language of instruction. Students of those universities will thus be expected to develop their academic writing skills in English, and they may not be competent in academic writing in their mother tongue. Indeed, some languages may not have developed the required terminology necessary for academic writing. So, there is no option but to use English. For students who have been taught in this way, it is perhaps misleading to say that they use English as an *additional* language, when it is the default as far as writing is concerned. Nevertheless, we will use this term, as it is the preferred one in ERPP studies.

Other things being equal, and in spite of the variations between different types of EAL writers, it is likely that EAL writers, at least when they are novices, will find it more difficult when it comes to writing for publication than their Anglophone counterparts. Issues of equity thus arise. It is not that Anglophone writers do not find it difficult when it comes to academic writing; academic writing presents challenges for Anglophones as well. Indeed, for this reason, some have argued that "academic language is … no one's mother tongue" (Bourdieu, Passeron, & Saint Martin, 1994, p. 8). It is just that there are additional challenges for EAL writers. These challenges, indeed, have been the driving force behind the development of ERPP, making it a political movement for some, as well as a field of academic enquiry. This dimension of ERPP will be dealt with in greater detail in the chapters to come.

Conclusion

In this chapter we have highlighted the emergence and nature of the culture and ideology of publish or perish in current academia, the fact that it has put scholars at all levels under extensive pressure in many academic contexts, and its implications for scholars and scholarly publication globally. We have stressed the importance of an understanding of the global socio–political and socio–economic and ideological factors which have brought this situation about. Some of the enumerated factors include the sweep of globalisation and neoliberalisation of the academy and consequently strict regimes of evaluation and audit; the current status of English as the international medium of communication and consequently as the default medium of scholarly discourse and exchange for many multilingual scholars; the expansion and massification of higher education and growing number of tertiary education institutions; and the role of academic institutions as the impetus behind economic growth and expansion and as emblems of national pride and prestige. It should be noted, however, that this is not an exhaustive list of factors and other global and local policies, practices, and conditions have played an important role in the emergence and expansion of this culture. We have also pointed out that the culture of publish or perish is not equally spread across individual universities, academic systems, countries, or regions. Although we have dealt with these issues individually, they are in fact interdependent; we are talking about a confluence of macro factors, rather than a chain of cause and effect. Such a multivariant and multifaceted macro and micro understanding will contribute to developing strategies, policies, and practices that can help understand this phenomenon better and can alleviate the challenges that many scholars are facing in their attempts to contribute to the construction and dissemination of scholarship.

Note

1 https://en.wikipedia.org/wiki/Clarivate_Analytics

3

FROM THE SCIENTIFIC ENLIGHTENMENT TO PUBLISH OR PERISH

Introduction

Over millennia, different languages have been used in scientific communication, the major ones being Aramaic, Greek, Arabic, Latin, French, German, and English (Hamel, 2007). Also, in non-Western traditions, important early scientific discoveries have been recorded in Chinese and other languages (Bodde, 1991). However, as described in Chapter 2, especially since the Second World War, English has come to dominate, so that the great majority of important scientific findings are reported in English. In the first part of this chapter, we will describe the historical development of scientific communication in English since the Enlightenment. We feel that a historical perspective is an important dimension of ERPP as a field, because it can provide a deeper understanding of how scientific communication has arrived at the publish or perish situation we are in now, as we have described in the previous chapter, and will continue to discuss in more detail in the rest of this book. Put simply, an understanding of the past can help understand the present. In this chapter, we will see how the research article (RA) has come to be the preeminent vehicle for the reporting of science in international scholarly communication. We will also describe some of its rhetorical contours and linguistic properties and features. After that, we will briefly look at the historical development of peer review as a scholarship adjudication and certification process in academia. We will also consider some evaluation metrics which have developed to assess the quality of journals and individual scholars' research performance, as measured by publications, in more recent times. We will see how we have come a very long way since the early days of the Scientific Enlightenment of the 17th and 18th centuries.

DOI: 10.4324/9780429317798-3

The Enlightenment as the foundation of modern scientific inquiry

Empirical science as we know it today developed during the period known as the Enlightenment in the 17th and 18th centuries in Europe. Prior to that, knowledge of the world and codes of conduct were based on revealed knowledge, that is to say, knowledge based on the authority of a higher power, be that the Christian Church or the divine right of kings and queens. Subjects under such regimes based their decisions on religious beliefs and all matters were interpreted in light of this dogma. If something did not fit in with the system of beliefs, then it was discounted or considered to be heretical.

Enlightenment scholars, including the continental rationalist philosophers Descartes, Spinoza, and Leibniz, the British empirical philosophers Locke, Berkeley, and Hume, and men (sic) of science, as empirical scientists were referred to at the time, such as Copernicus, Galileo, Bacon, and Newton, based their theories on rational knowledge. Beliefs had to be based on reason, not just on what had been passed down by the Church. Theories needed to be based on demonstrable, fact-based data to support their conclusions. If the facts did not fit the theory, then the theory was wrong or needed to be adapted.

Accompanying these ideas was a revolution in practical science, the so-called scientific revolution, which took the form of a series of developments in mathematics, physics, astronomy, biology, and chemistry. Landmark theories developed as part of this revolution are Copernicus's *De revolutionibus orbium coelestium* (*On the revolutions of the heavenly spheres*), Galileo's *Dialogue concerning the two chief world systems* (translated from Italian into Latin as *Systema cosmicum*), and Newton's *Philosophiæ naturalis principia mathematica* (translated from Latin into English as *Mathematical principles of natural philosophy*), which formulated the laws of motion and gravity. Many of the Enlightenment scientists worked with experimental and mathematical methods. In support of such approaches, Francis Bacon (1620/1848, p. 345) famously wrote that "intellect, left to itself, ought always to be suspected". Such empirical approaches gradually led to a more or less established procedure for scientific inquiry, the so-called scientific method. This involved making hypotheses, making predictions based on these hypotheses, and testing the hypotheses by means of experiments in order to determine if observations match up with or disagree with the hypotheses. This approach, although perhaps an idealisation and not followed in all cases, can be set out as the following stages:

Research question > Hypothesis > Prediction > Experiment > Analysis

This process is relevant to this book because it prefigures the typical pattern for reporting research in the form of the RA, with its so-called IMRaD format of:

Introduction > Method > Results > Discussion

We will consider this pattern in more detail later.

Development of scientific communication from the Enlightenment onwards

Enlightenment philosophers and scientists disseminated and discussed their ideas through meetings at coffee houses, literary salons, masonic lodges, scientific societies, and academies (Weber, 1992). France, England, Germany, Russia, and Denmark all had scientific societies or academies with royal or government patrons (Gunnarsson, 2011, p. 5). The Royal Society in London was established in 1660 with King Charles II as patron. The Académie Royale des Sciences in Paris was founded in 1666, under the patronage of Colbert, the minister of finance.

Early written scientific communication took the form of letters which scientists wrote to each other. In fact, this practice is still reflected in many present-day scientific journals which have the term *letters* in their title, although the scientific letter has become a particular genre in the present day: a short report often published more quickly than a full RA and reflecting innovative and/or more newsworthy work (Hyland, 2009). The following are some examples selected at random to represent a number of disciplines: *Applied Economics Letters, Chemistry Letters, Ecology Letters, IEEE Electron Device Letters*, and *Physical Review Letters*. The letters were written in a polite style, and typically addressed several subjects at the same time (Kronick, 1976). In the 17th and 18th centuries, scientific letters mainly took the form of descriptive narratives structured chronologically, although there was no generally accepted format (Meadows, 1985). During the early Enlightenment period, the common language for written scientific communication was Latin, which allowed for an international approach to scientific inquiry. Gradually, however, vernacular languages became fully acceptable alternatives. Thus, as indicated above, Galileo's *Dialogue concerning the two chief world systems* was originally written in Italian and then translated to Latin. Newton's *Prinicipia*, on the other hand, was first written in Latin and then translated into English.

In order to disseminate scientific ideas as widely as possible, the newly established societies and academies established periodicals. The first scientific journal, *Journal des sçavans*, was published in France in January 1665. The most influential early journal, however, which quickly followed on the heels of the *Journal des sçavans*, was the Royal Society's *Philosophical Transactions*, which also began publishing in 1665, but in March, two months later than the *Journal des sçavans*. Under its first editor, Henry Oldenburg, contributions were published in the *Philosophical Transactions* from Isaac Newton, Robert Boyle, Christopher Wren, and Robert Hooke, among many others. The *Transactions*, from the outset, was an international journal, with contributions from and distributed in many European countries, although many of the contributors and readers were English, and, apart from some early submissions in Latin, the language of publication was English (McDougall-Waters, Moxham, & Fyfe, 2015). Oldenburg had a vast network of acquaintances among the intellectuals and natural philosophers in Europe. He was also an accomplished linguist, writing fluently in English, Dutch, French, German, Italian, and Latin. He was in fact what nowadays would be referred to as a plurilingual scholar (Englander & Corcoran, 2019).

An influential member of the Royal Society was Robert Boyle, most famous for his experiments with the wind pump. Boyle was also very influential with regard to scientific discourse and modes of communication (Shapin, 1984; Shapin & Schaffer, 1985). He maintained that experiments should be witnessed by peers (in his case, members of the Royal Society), in order to establish their credibility and the assent of the scientific community. They could then be reported in written form for unlimited dissemination. Boyle argued that the author of a scientific report should strive to create in the mind's eye of the reader a visual representation of the experiment. Only in this way could "matters of fact" be established. This was done by detailed descriptions of methods and detailed images of the equipment used, features which were to later develop as standard features of the RA. To further establish the credibility of science, accounts were also included of experiments which had failed. In addition, modesty of speech was required, to further establish the writer as a reliable witness and that what was reported was an unclouded mirror of nature. A *functional*, as opposed to a *florid*, style was to be adopted with the same goal in mind. While for "matters of fact", assertive language was to be used, where conjecture and speculation were concerned, hesitancy was required. Thus, Boyle told his nephew:

> in almost every one of the following essays I … speak so doubtingly, and use so often, *perhaps, it seems, it is not improbable,* and such other expressions, as argue a diffidence of the truth of the opinions I incline to, and that I should be so shy of laying down principles, and sometimes of so much as venturing at explications.
>
> *Reported in Shapin, 1984, p. 495*

Many of these features recommended by Boyle have remained or developed further as characteristics of the RA to the present day (Gil-Salom & Soler-Monreal, 2009; Hyland, 1998a, 1998b; Latour & Woolgar, 1986; Myers, 1989). Myers (1989), for example, identifies various politeness features in scientific RAs, such as pronouns and passives which are used to avoid threatening the face of the reader (Brown & Levinson, 1987) and certain adverbs used to create a sense of solidarity with the reader (Brown & Levinson, 1987), to draw the reader in. Hyland (1998b) describes the role of *boosters* and *hedges* in scientific text. Boosters are rhetorical strategies designed to emphasise conviction and confidence in a statement and are expressed by adverbs such as *clearly, obviously,* and *of course.* Like Myers's (1989) politeness features, they are designed to create a sense of solidarity with the reader. Hedges, on the other hand, are rhetorical strategies designed to reduce the force of a statement and are realised by modality markers such as *possible, might,* and *perhaps.* They are the antithesis of boosters, reducing a writer's commitment to a statement and expressing an element of doubt. Together boosters and hedges allow the sense of decorum and politeness in scientific discourse argued for by Boyle.

The research article as the preeminent genre for the international scholar

The preeminent genre in which scholars seek to publish for most disciplines today is the RA. Some humanities and social science (HSS) disciplines have traditionally preferred full-length books, or monographs, although under pressure from research assessment bodies, they have been increasingly moving towards RAs (Hyland, 2009). Edited collections of articles, where each chapter is the responsibility of a different author or group of authors, with an editor controlling the scope of the volume and usually writing an introduction, are also popular in the HSS disciplines. Scholars may also need to write other genres, such as research proposals, reports, book reviews, and online blogs, which are becoming popular. However, it is the RA which is the measure of esteem that the great majority of scholars focus their main attention on. There are also some complementary, facilitating genres, such as resumes and curricula vita (CVs), cover letters for journal submissions, and emails. The ability to write effectively (in English) in all of these genres is important in the career of any scholar, but they are not in and of themselves important for the level of esteem or otherwise in which a scholar is held.

Although there was no standard form for articles in the early journals, and reports of experiments were simple chronological descriptions, the scientific article gradually developed into a more structured format, with methods and results increasingly described and interpreted, so that by the second half of the 19th century a pattern of "theory–experiment–discussion" became conventional (Atkinson, 1999). By the early part of the 20th century, the IMRaD structure was established (Bazerman, 1988), although it did not become the accepted standard until the 1970s, when, in 1972 and again in 1979, the American national standard for the preparation of scientific papers for written or oral presentation (ANSI Z39.16-1972) was published (Day, 1989). A great many natural science disciplines follow this pattern, although it is not obligatory. HSS disciplines, where research does not depend upon experiments and hence "results", may not follow the IMRaD pattern and there is greater freedom of how to structure an RA. Review articles are another special case, where no "results" are included. Some natural science disciplines also have their preferred RA structures which deviate from IMRaD. Maths RAs, for example, eschew Method and Results sections for a simpler Introduction–Results model; Graves, Moghaddasi, and Hashim (2013) argue that this simpler, more succinct structure is more suited to the well-established maths methodology, which is based on deduction and induction and does not need explanations of Method or Discussion of findings.

A study by Lin and Evans (2012) of 433 recent empirical RAs from high-impact English-language journals in 39 disciplines in the fields of engineering, applied sciences, social sciences, and the humanities found that although IMRaD is a very common pattern, it is not the default. The most frequently used structural pattern is in fact Introduction–Literature Review–Method–Results and

Discussion–Conclusion (ILM[RD]C) (with IMRaD articles, the Literature Review would be included as part of the Introduction). Other frequent patterns found in Lin and Evans's (2012) corpus are IM[RD]C, IMRDC, ILMRDC, and ILMRD. These patterns thus include a merged Results and Discussion (RD), a separate Literature Review (L), and a separate Conclusion (C).

Whatever preferred pattern a discipline or sub-discipline may have, a predictable organisation allows the reader to find the information that they need efficiently, even if the reporting sequence does not actually correspond to the sequence of events of the actual research process. Readers do not read RAs from beginning to end, but scan the article for the information that they require. A predictable structure facilitates this process. From the point of view of the author, a conventional modular structure allows for an efficient organisation of ideas and facilitates the writing process. As for editors and reviewers, a template helps in the evaluation process, which in turn will assist the author, because the review can be written using the same organisational structure.

The discursive make-up of the RA has developed in various ways since the time of Robert Boyle and the Royal Society (Mack, 2012). There has been a shift away from the personal narrative reported in chronological order towards an impersonal account following IMRaD, with a heavy use of the passive voice and other impersonal grammatical devices. It is the voice of science speaking rather than the voice of the individual scientist – indeed, many if not most RAs are nowadays multiple-authored. While Boyle and the Royal Society sought to publish articles that could be read by the educated public, nowadays there is much more disciplinary specialisation and technical vocabularies have developed. There has also been a move towards lengthy noun phrases to express a concept, where previously a verbal construction would have been preferred, a process referred to as nominalisation (Halliday, 2004). Halliday (2004) provides the following pair of sentences to demonstrate this progression (the first is a more verbal construction and the second is more nominal [nominalisations highlighted]):

1. Grass cracks more quickly the harder you press it.
2. **Glass crack growth rate** is associated with **applied stress magnitude**. (p. 113)

Boyle emphasised the use of hedging for speculative language and indeed this has greatly increased in the scientific writing of today, with authors careful to signal degrees of certainty and doubt, on the one hand, and probability and possibility, on the other. Boyle emphasised the importance of images of the equipment used in experiments, but, in those days, they were extremely expensive to make (they were based on engravings) and were used sparingly (Boyle was an exceptionally rich man, so he could afford to have them produced). Today's journal articles are replete with figures and tables, often presenting quantitative data, which did not feature in the 17th century. In Boyle's time, it was rare to cite another publication, but, over the centuries, citation has become increasingly frequent, with almost every journal article now including references on an increasing scale (Mack, 2012). Of course, this is facilitated by the fact that, with the explosion in publication, there is much more other research available to refer to. We will discuss the structure and linguistic features of the RA in much more detail in later chapters.

Peer review

Early on in the history of the Royal Society's *Transactions* journal, the editor Henry Oldenberg was concerned to establish the reputation of the journal and the Society. He was also aware that publication of an article conferred prestige on a contributor and legitimacy to their words and he was therefore careful in how he sourced submissions. He accordingly vetted articles he commissioned carefully and had members of the Society who were knowledgeable on the topic review them. The *Journal des sçavans* adopted a similar policy in France. This was the beginning of the process which came to be referred to as *peer review*. A precursor of peer review was recommended by Ishāq ibn 'Alī al-Ruhāwī (854–931) in his *The ethics of the physician* (Spier, 2002). He argued that a visiting physician should make a duplicate set of notes of a patient's condition on every visit so that after a patient's treatment was finished, the notes of the physician could be examined by a medical council of other doctors in order to evaluate whether the treatment was appropriate.

Peer review (also known as *refereeing*) is the process by which an RA, book, or other type of manuscript intended for publication is vetted by experts who are specialists in the same field. The goal of peer review is to assist editors and publishers in deciding if a manuscript is suitable or has potential for publication. It can filter out papers with "irrelevant, trivial, weak, misleading, or potentially harmful content" while at the same time "improving the clarity, transparency, accuracy, and utility" of potential papers (Larson & Chung, 2012, p. 38). It plays an important role in building the reputation of individual scientists and of science as a social enterprise, while certifying the quality and reliability of research findings (Moxham & Fyfe, 2017). On the other hand, peer review as a fair and efficient way of evaluating and disseminating scientific knowledge has its critics. We will discuss some of the criticisms in Chapter 7, when we will discuss peer review in more detail.

Impact factor

Let us return to the concept of impact factor, mentioned in previous chapters. Impact factor is a measure of the frequency with which the average article in a journal has been cited in a particular year. Table 3.1 was downloaded from the website of the University of Texas medical library (Gann, 2020). It shows impact factor data of the 12,298 journals tracked by the *Journal Citation Reports* (JCR) database of the Web of Science in 2017. Of these journals, 239 (1.9%) had an impact factor of 10 or higher. The top 5% of journals had impact factors approximately equal to or greater than 6 (610, or 4.9%). Approximately two-thirds of the journals had an impact factor equal to or greater than 1. On the other hand, extrapolating

TABLE 3.1 Impact factor data of the 12,298 journals tracked by the *Journal Citation Reports* (JCR) database of the Web of Science in 2017

Impact Factor	Number of Journals	Ranking (Top % of Journals)
10+	239	1.9%
9+	290	2.4%
8+	356	2.9%
7+	447	3.6%
6+	610	4.9%
5+	871	7.1%
4+	1,399	11.4%
3+	2,575	21%
2+	4,840	39.4%
1+	8,757	71.2%
0+	12,298	100%

from these figures, the table shows that nearly 30% of the journals included had an impact factor of less than 1.

Impact factor can therefore be a good metric for ranking journals according to the set criteria. It must be borne in mind, however, that not all journals have impact factors – because they are not included in the Web of Science (see Chapter 2) or have not been publishing long enough to be included. Furthermore, as reported by Englander (2014), only 11.6 % of the journals that are included in the Web of Science publish in a language that is not English (Brunner-Ried & Salazar-Muñiz, 2012), suggesting that there must be many such journals which are left out. In short, there is a lot of research being conducted that is not getting widely reported and evaluated.

Authorship

At the time of Henry Oldenberg, scientists published individually. Since then, however, there has been an increasing trend for scholars to do collaborative work and towards co-authorship. Hyland (2015) points out that there is considerable variation in co-authorship patterns across disciplines. Experimental sciences such as high-energy physics have an average of nine authors per paper, while theoretical sciences have fewer, with physics and computer science averaging three co-authors. In the social sciences, where there is co-authoring, two co-authors is the norm, but single authoring is more common.

In cases of co-authoring, care is needed in the ordering in which the names are listed. It is important that there should be agreement in the ordering of the names at an early stage, so as to pre-empt potential disputes later. Casanave (1998) reports a difficult co-authoring experience of a Japanese scholar with her former US PhD supervisor, having to decide "who would be listed as first author, who would draft and revise, and generally how to balance the work of preparing an article for publication" (p. 191). The default order is to list names alphabetically. Where this is the case, the contributions may be assumed to be equal. If the names are not listed alphabetically, then the order indicates that the contributions are different. That is, if the authors are X followed by Y, the default reading here is that X and Y contributed equally. If, on the other hand, the listing is Y followed by X, then the assumption is that Y contributed more than X. An exception is where two authors collaborate on a number of papers and decide to alternate the ordering of their names each time that they publish a paper. Where the default of X followed by Y occurs, it is not always the case, however, that contributions are in fact equal. In such a situation, there is no doubt that X has contributed at least 50%, but it may be more than that and Y may have contributed less. There is an apparent advantage to be had if one's name begins with an early letter in the alphabet, Abbot, for example, because it is more likely to come first in default situations. On the other hand, if one's name begins with a letter occurring later in the alphabet, Zhang, for example, in situations where one's contribution has been less than 50%, readers may be misled into assuming that the contribution has been equal, that is to say, more than in fact is the case.

As the number of co-authors increases beyond two, the meaning of position becomes increasingly arbitrary (Tscharntke, Hochberg, Rand, Resh, & Krauss, 2007). Avula and Avula (2015) write as follows on this:

> The last author often gets as much credit as the first author, because he or she is assumed to be the driving force, both intellectually and financially, behind the research. Evaluation committees and funding bodies often take last authorship as a sign of successful group leadership and make this a criterion in hiring, granting, and promotion. This practice is unofficial, and hence not always followed, meaning that sometimes last authors "mistakenly" benefit when they actually are not principal investigators. Moreover, there is no accepted yardstick in assessing the actual contribution of a group leader to given scientific publications, so interpretation of author sequence can be like a lottery. Hence, one really does not know if being last author means that the overall contribution was the most or least important.

Clearly, the interpretation of the listing of authors on research papers is a minefield for evaluators, and it is difficult in many cases to know how to assign due credit. As a result, some journals now require authors to indicate the percentage of contributions on their paper, which is a step in the right direction. But it may be difficult even for the authors to decide on relative contributions. What value is to be attached to the person designing the study, to the one conducting the actual experiments, to the one doing the statistics, to the one running the laboratory in which the research was conducted, or to the one doing the writing? There are, furthermore, power issues at stake. Senior academics may apply pressure on junior colleagues to include their name on a publication undeservedly or to falsely represent their percentage of contribution. It is ironic that such a situation should subsist in today's marketised universities. Markets are supposed to put a price on everything and operate fairly, but clearly, as with other aspects of the publication process, this is not the case.

Publication output

With the increasing pressure to publish, it is more and more difficult to achieve publication in the top journals (although, as mentioned in Chapter 1, there are many more journals, which make publication easier, but not in the top journals). Schultz (2009) reports that the rejection rate of submissions to the 46 atmospheric science journals in 2006 ranged from 2% to 68%, with a mean of 37%. As authors of this book, this does not seem so bad for us. However, Khadilkar (2018) reports that rejection rates for various top-tier journals (those with the highest impact factors) vary between 80 and 85% and that some journals (he cites three top medical journals: *The Lancet*, *The New England Journal of Medicine*, and *The Journal of the American Medical Association*) have reported their rejection rates to be around 90–95%. This does not surprise us at all.

So, if it is very difficult to publish, what sort of output are we talking about for the average scholar? This is a very difficult question to answer, because, apart from the competence of the scholar, it depends on a wide range of factors, including the following:

- The discipline a scholar is working in (HSS scholars tend to publish less, but the length of their articles tends to be longer, and they may write monographs).
- Whether publications are single-authored or multi-authored. Many HSS scholars like to work on their own, but by no means all. On the other hand, scholars in the STEM disciplines, who tend to do laboratory-based research, may work in what can be very large teams under the supervision of the director of the laboratory, with many names appearing on each publication. Such authors will likely have many more publications than authors who publish alone.
- What type of university a scholar is based in. Prestigious research universities tend to expect more publications than their less prestigious counterparts, so there is more pressure, but usually better conditions for doing research.

Within disciplines and universities, publication rates tend to be skewed. One study of publication rates of 31,034 Italian academics in 192 "hard science" fields across 86 Italian universities (Abramo & D'Angelo, 2015) found in the subset of 554 academics in the field of organic chemistry that 10% of those scholars surveyed had produced on average less than one publication per year, and six were totally unproductive. On the other hand, 20 individuals within this field had over 10 publications per year, with one outlier at over 25 publications per year. These figures are normalised to take account of multi-authored papers, so the results include fractional papers. Although these numbers are not without interest, such analyses are flawed, because, in spite of measures to allow for different fractions of contributions, these measures are not accurate. When some RAs have hundreds or even thousands of authors, usually listed alphabetically, it is impossible to calculate the relative contribution of each, just as it would be ridiculous to assign all of the citations to each of those authors (Belikov & Belikov, 2015). Similarly, a researcher who uses a particular piece of equipment to conduct experiments and is cited by all other researchers who subsequently use that equipment probably does not deserve those citations just because they previously used the equipment (Belikov & Belikov, 2015).

H-index

One increasingly popular metric for measuring and comparing productivity of individual scholars is the *h-index* or *h-factor*, invented by Hirsch (2005) (the "h" is the first letter in Hirsch's name). The h-index of an individual scholar is based on the number of their papers and the number of times those papers have been cited (Oswald, 2009). The advantage of this approach is that it takes account of both the number of articles published and their impact, as measured by the number of citations. It means that if you just have a few papers with very many citations or a large number of papers with few (or zero) citations, your h-index will be low. To be rewarded with a high h-index, you need to publish a high number of articles with a high number of citations. Both consistency and impact are thus important. Hirsch demonstrated the value of his measure (which was designed with only physics in mind) by showing that Nobel prize winners in physics all had high h-indices (84% had an h of at least 30). Hirsch estimated that for a physicist with 20 years of publishing, an H- index of 20 is good, 40 is outstanding, and 60 is exceptional.

So, it would seem that with the h-index we have a measure for comparing scholars' research output, at least across a single discipline. However, there are drawbacks with this method too. First, disciplines are not homogeneous. Within disciplines there are different specialisations. Some of these will be more popular areas than others. In medicine, for example, anything to do with COVID-19 at the time of writing is likely to be of interest to many scholars worldwide and therefore quite likely to be cited. Some areas of medicine are very much niche areas, however; some rare conditions are not exciting much, if any, research interest and so a scholar working in one of these areas is unlikely to acquire many citations, no matter how good the quality of their research might be. Second, some famous researchers, such as Isaac Newton, Gregor Mendel, or Peter Higgs, published only a few papers, which would give them very low h-indices of 4, 1, and 9, respectively, which even a mediocre junior scholar might be expected to achieve today (Belikov & Belikov, 2015). This seems counter-intuitive. At one university the authors of this book are familiar with and which puts great store by metrics (measures of quantitative assessment), when selecting new appointments, there was a saying that Einstein would never have been hired, because his h-index would not have been high enough. Third, there remains the problem of multi-authored papers. Fewer authors listed on an article should mean greater credit for those included, but this is not the case. Fourth, the h-index does not take into account length of publishing career. Other things being equal, more experienced scholars will have higher h-indexes (because they have published more articles), even if their junior colleagues are publishing better quality articles, but have not had time to accumulate either the required number of articles or the required number of citations for each article (bearing in mind that citations accumulate over time). Fifth, because review articles are generally cited more frequently than empirical studies, they have a greater impact on the h-index than the latter.

As with the impact factor, then, h-index is an imperfect system, but probably the best one available at the present time for the task it has set itself. As Hirsch himself wrote:

> Obviously, a single number can never give more than a rough approximation to an individual's multifaceted profile, and many other factors should be considered in combination in evaluating an individual. This and the fact that there can always be exceptions to rules should be kept in mind especially in life-changing decision such as the granting or denying of tenure.
>
> *2005, p. 16569*

Finally, there is an ethical dimension to the h-index. Some may argue that it is a dehumanising and demeaning process. As such, the h-index can be viewed as a manifestation of the neoliberalisation of the academy referred to in the previous chapter, with its strict regimes of audit and assessment.

Conclusion

In this chapter, we have considered the rise of empirical science from the 17th century Enlightenment, the development of scientific communication from the Enlightenment onwards, the development of the RA as the preeminent research genre, and some rhetorical and linguistic features of the RA. We then looked at some ways of ensuring and measuring publication quality. Accordingly, we focused on the development of peer review as a gatekeeping and knowledge evaluation process, Given the significance of academic productivity in the survival and visibility of academics, we also looked at how decisions regarding the assignment of authorship and authorship order are made and shared some conventional norms and strategies in that respect. We next discussed two key indexes, namely impact factor and h-factor, that are currently used to assess the quality of academic journals and academics, respectively, and their role and significance in stratification of both academic venues and scholars in the neoliberal evaluation-based academy of today. In what we covered, we have seen that since the 17th century, empirical science has always been concerned with rationality and credibility. More recently, alongside the publish or perish ethos, a culture of surveillance has developed in which the research performance of individual scholars and universities is constantly measured and ranked. Monahan (2011, p. 498) defines surveillance as "the systematic monitoring of people or groups in order to regulate or control their behaviour". When applied to individuals, this quantitative and commodifying process, if not moderated sensitively with more qualitative and collegial measures, is demeaning in itself, but when the monitoring used in this process is not accurate, it can become even more pernicious. We have certainly come a long way from the witnessing of experiments of Robert Boyle.

4

DISCOURSES AND PERSPECTIVES ON ENGLISH

Introduction

In Chapter 2, we considered the global forces giving rise to the phenomenon of publish or perish, including Global English, and in Chapter 3 we considered how the research article (RA) as we know it today developed out of 17th century Enlightenment science and how various evaluative practices have developed since then alongside it. Given the important role that English has played in these systems and developments, in this chapter, we will examine some of the discourses, discussions, and perspectives with regard to English as a Global Language and their application in ERPP research. We will first consider two important, contrasting discourses on English – the *laissez-faire*, liberal discourse and the *linguistic imperialism* discourse (Pennycook, 2000). We will discuss the underlying assumptions of these discourses on the emergence, spread, and role of English as a Global Language. We will look at how these discourses have extended to and informed the use of English as a site of struggle in ERPP discussions and affected ERPP scholarship. We will then consider the notion of *domain loss* and how the dominant status of Global English in academic discourse and exchange may endanger and threaten the existence and role of other academic languages. Following these more theoretical sections, we will move on to see how these different discourses and perspectives have been reflected in ERPP studies, in particular in the debate concerning linguistic inequality in the construction and communication of knowledge and the contested topic of the disadvantaged position of EAL scholars in the field of writing for publication in English. Finally, we will discuss the place and implications of World Englishes and English as a Lingua Franca in ERPP studies and scholarship.

DOI: 10.4324/9780429317798-4

Discourses around English

One of the key elements in ERPP scholarship and the impetus behind its emergence and expansion is the significance of the medium in which scholarly production is carried out in today's academy, that is to say, English. The historical rise and spread of English across the globe and its usage in all aspects of modern life, including in the academy, has been the subject of a huge literature emerging from language studies, postcolonial studies, language policy studies, and, to a lesser extent, political studies. It is important for ERPP scholars to understand the competing discourses in this field, as whichever is drawn upon will inform their attitudes to writing for publication in English.

Pennycook (2000) enumerates a number of different perspectives that can frame an understanding of the global position of English, of which two, "*laissez-faire* liberalism" and "linguistic imperialism", have influenced and informed ERPP scholarship. The difference between these two views is basically in how they conceptualise the role of language in human interactions and how it is connected with broader cultural, political, ideological, and identity issues. In what follows, we will take a look at some of the theoretical and discoursal underpinnings of these two attitudes towards the spread of English.

Laissez-faire liberalism

The first perspective, *laissez-faire* liberalism, adopts a cosmopolitanist, liberal, instrumental, pragmatic, and apolitical view of English as a neutral beneficial *lingua franca* (e.g., Crystal, 2003; de Swaan, 2001a, 2001b; Van Parijs, 2004). According to this discourse, English plays a positive, unifying role in international communication and intelligibility. In addition to the term *laissez-faire* itself, this discourse employs a range of other metaphors from the field of economics; it is a *commodity* no longer tied to a specific geopolitical context and which belongs to all human beings; it is a global *currency* that can be exchanged on global markets; it provides invaluable social, symbolic, and material *capitals* for those who possess it; and it promises *prestige, development*, and *prosperity* to those who use it. Furthermore, Global English, according to this *laissez-faire* discourse, is a democratic force, empowering those who learn it or interact in it and giving voice to the voiceless or the under-heard. It is thus an important component of neoliberal discourse, as sketched out in Chapter 2.

Global English, according to this discourse, has not come about as the result of some premeditated plan, or conspiracy, but is the result of "unintended consequences of a myriad of individual decisions" (de Swaan, 2001a, p. 186) and "countless uncoordinated choices" (Van Parijs, 2004, p. 148). As Kaplan (2001) argues:

> It is unlikely that there is some grand conspiracy among English-speakers to disseminate English world-wide; on the contrary, the spread of English is largely accidental, based in part on the quest for an allegedly better standard

of living on the part of receiving populations, and in part on the unconscious press of English on other populations.

p. 17

And, as Crystal (2003) states, "[t]he English language has already grown to be independent of any form of social control" (p. 190). Its use is the result of a rational choice on the part of users, not some sort of imposition.

Finally, as a result of the above arguments, the *laissez-faire* discourse:

> suggests that we should not engage in ideological/political discussions of language and that we should make freedom of choice our central mode of understanding. Everyone is free to do what they like with English, to use English in beneficial ways and to use other languages for other purposes.
>
> *Pennycook, 2000, p. 111*

As applied to the academy, the *laissez-faire* discourse implies a neutral, beneficial position for English in the creation and maintenance of international communities of scholars. English offers more benefits than costs for academics globally and facilitates international communication and academic exchange among scholars, a role that was once carried out by another language, Latin. The spread of English in the global academy, as with other fields of Global English, "is essentially a coincidence of the confluence of a number of political and economic forces during the last half of the 20th century" (Kaplan, 2001, p. 1). In any case, "[c]learly, the advantages of English as a world language of social science are too precious, both for individual scholars and for the science community in its entirety, to relinquish" (de Swaan, 2001b, p. 79). Finally, because of these benefits, the role of English should not be questioned:

> Based on a mixture of general political liberalism and more specific academic apoliticism — a view that academic work should somehow remain neutral — this approach will either deny ideological implications of the global spread of English, or suggest that they are not our concern.
>
> *Pennycook, 2000, p. 109*

Linguistic imperialism

Critics of the *laissez-faire* discourse on Global English find it very simplistic and reductionist. They argue that the apolitical, uncritical, and unideological narratives presented in works such as those of Kaplan (2001) and Crystal (2003) about the rise and hegemony of English separates the communicative aspect of English from its historical and socio-political underpinnings and determinants and "conflates the *process* and *project*" of Englicization (Phillipson, 2009, p. 110, emphasis in the original). In other words, this narrative does not consider the role of colonialism in the emergence of English as an international language, the socio-economic and political factors and cultural policies in its promotion and sustenance as the inter-national language, and the centripetal (and centrifugal) forces that have played an important role in the emergence and expansion of English (see Pennycook, 1998; Phillipson, 1992).

Turning now to the second of the two approaches to Global English posited by Pennycook (2000), linguistic imperialism, this perspective is the polar opposite of *laissez-faire*. As such, it takes a less internationalistic, more sceptical, and critical view of English and its expansion and role in the modern world. In this view, English is not an innocent, neutral, all-beneficial medium of interaction. It is a language with specific socio-political, economic, and cultural agendas, and extensive and growing hegemonic power; it is an "'imperialist', 'predatory' or 'killer' language that threatens linguistic diversity" (Ives, 2006, pp. 121–122). *Pandemic* (Phillipson & Skutnabb-Kangas, 1994), *Lingua Frankensteinia* (Phillipson, 2008), and *Lingua Tyrannosaura* (Swales, 1997) are some of the terms used to describe Global English in this perspective, all terms with highly negative connotations.

Unlike the first *laissez-faire* view, this perspective on English brings to the fore the political, ideological, power, and identity issues concerned with language and does not regard English and its spread as a merely neutral communicative tool. From this perspective, the hierarchisation of languages, the ascendency and hegemony of English in all aspects and domains of the modern world, and its undermining effects on other languages is not a random and accidental phenomenon. It is the result of a calculated scheme that has its roots in the colonial and imperial era. The current status of English is due to the political and economic power of the US and the UK, serving their (neo)imperialist and (neo)colonialist objectives, and guaranteeing their cultural, political, and economic hegemony across the globe (Pennycook, 1994; Phillipson, 1992, 2009).

Finding the middle ground

So, is there a middle way between the highly contrastive discourses on English we have just sketched out? There is no doubt that the status, role, and function of a language cannot be explained and analysed "without a fairly deeper understanding of the sociohistorical context within which it has evolved" (Ricento, 2000, p. 1) and an acceptance of the fact that "language policies are always socially situated" (Ricento, 2000, p. 4). Those adhering to a more moderate paradigm generally agree that the current status of English poses threats to other languages and their role and position in the global linguistic landscape, although the degree of criticality and, more importantly, the extent to which (neo)imperialist and (neo)colonialist motives are claimed to underlie the spread of English differ (Phillipson, 2009). Although this critical perspective highlights the socio-politics of language policy and use, as Ammon (2007) argues, the proponents of the linguistic imperialism view should take into account the fact that the effects of direct language promotion, as such, are actually quite limited. He makes the point that Francophone countries have been equally keen to promote their language as their Anglophone counterparts, but have not been equally successful, because of a lack of resources and promise, including science, that a global language needs in order to be successful. In sum, as Guardiano, Favilla, and Calaresu (2007) argue, it seems that "no answer to the problem posed by the dominance of English can be satisfactorily provided unless we overcome the same stereotyped dichotomy of English as a 'language killer' and English as a kind of 'communicative cure-all'" (p. 49). With this in mind, we will now look at the implications of these discourses and discussion for ERPP scholarship and research orientations.

Domain loss

An important reason for guarding against the hegemony of English is so-called *domain loss*, the loss of language use in certain domains and genres due to them being overtaken by English (Ferguson, 2007). This tends to occur in the high-prestige domains of higher education, scientific communication, and transnational business (Ferguson, 2007; Laurén, 2002). It is what Swales means when he refers to English as *Tyrannosaurus Rex*, "a powerful carnivore gobbling up the other denizens of the academic linguistic grazing grounds" (Swales, 1997, p. 374). As Bordet (2016) has noted, if scientific innovation is created in only one language, English, then other languages and cultures are precluded from developing their own conceptualisations through "their native lexico-semantic patterns" (p. 2), a process Bennett (2015) refers to as *epistemicide*. This may lead to "a general impoverishment of thinking and creativity due to the domination of the Anglophone world's epistemological patterns, with the concomitant loss of specialized terminology, or domain loss, in languages other than English" (p. 2). On another level, if all international journals publish in English and follow Anglo-American discursive norms, they may discriminate against the discursive norms of EAL scholars from other language backgrounds and reject what are perceived to be linguistic idiosyncrasies, or "non-standard" English (Ammon, 2000; de Swaan, 2001b), including patterns of argumentation. Finally, an important practical (and moral) reason in scientific research and publication for wanting to guard against domain loss concerns the dissemination of scientific knowledge to local communities, so-called knowledge transfer. In applied fields, such as nursing or agriculture, knowledge needs to be passed on to technicians, health workers, and farmers operating in those domains, who may not have the high levels of competence in English that academics do (Flowerdew, 2013a). Di Bitetti and Ferreras (2017) explain this as follows:

> ...publishing scientific papers exclusively in English may limit the ability of non-NES [non-English-speaking] scientists to communicate important results to local practitioners and decision makers (e.g., environmental managers). This creates the moral dilemma of deciding whether to publish in English and making the results accessible to a broader audience or transferring knowledge to local experts.

They suggest that this dilemma could be resolved by following up on possibilities for bi- or multi- lingual publication of scientific papers (e.g., Meneghini & Packer, 2007; Root-Bernstein & Ladle, 2014), a call which has been taken up by some ERPP scholars (e.g., Corcoran & Englander, 2016; Englander & Corcoran, 2019). Some countries which have encouraged multilingualism in science and publication, e.g., the Nordic countries and Canada (Gentil & Séror, 2014; McGrath, 2016), have had only limited success in this initiative, however, because of conflicting signals. While some policies encourage publication in the national language, the assessment criteria emphasise publication in English (López-Navarro, Moreno, Quintanilla, & Rey-Rocha, 2015).

Global English and ERPP

Clearly, many disciplinary and ERPP scholars and practitioners may have conflicting attitudes towards the status and role of English and fall somewhere along the continuum between the two poles of *laissez-faire* liberalism and linguistic imperialism. Some may be quite happy to assent to the status quo, accepting that the role of ERPP is to facilitate research and publication in English and not to promote national languages. Others may be critical of the hegemonic nature of English and want to guard against it, including encouraging publishing in national languages rather than English, where possible and appropriate (Swales, 1997). This dichotomy applies also to students of ERPP. Some may be interested in discussing the ideologies behind writing for publication and Global English (see e.g., Cadman, 2017), while others may be disinterested, wanting to focus on the practicalities of achieving publication (see e.g., Flowerdew & Wang, 2017). Nevertheless, the hegemonic status of English has always been a major concern among many ERPP scholars, especially those on the critical side of the Global English spectrum (Ammon, 2007, 2016; Englander & Corcoran, 2019; Flowerdew, 2007; Swales, 1997, 2004). These concerns highlight the fact that a large part of ERPP scholarship and research has been informed and influenced by the ideological and political interpretation of the role and status of English.

EAL inequality

With the rise of English as the dominant language of research and publication and the fact that a majority of scholars now use English as an additional language, a question of equity arises. Clearly, it is likely to be more of a challenge to read and write for publication in an additional language than it is in one's mother tongue (Ammon, 2007, 2016; Flowerdew, 2019; La Madeleine, 2007). Van Parijs (2007) argues that Anglophone scholars have a "free ride" when it comes to writing for publication. While EAL writers have to spend time and money learning English, perhaps paying for help with the language and taking longer to read and write, their Anglophone counterparts spend little or nothing in terms of time or money, according to this argument (Ryazanova, McNamara, & Aguinis, 2017). Ferguson

(2007) uses the metaphor of "location rent" to address the same issue. Anglophones are sitting on a free resource, English, while EAL scholars have to pay in time, money, and effort in order to operate in what is for them an additional language. In a bibliometric survey involving over 3,000 institutions publishing in 149 high-impact business and management journals, Ryazanova, McNamara, and Aguinis (2017) found that business schools located in English-speaking countries dominated the rankings in terms of publication output, with 79 institutions in the top 100 and 146 institutions in the top 200:

> Business schools signal … quality [of their "research environment"] globally through research outputs which are predominantly published in English-language journals. This makes an institution's endowment of linguistic capital (i.e., the ability of faculty to write competently in academic English) a source of heterogeneity within the [business schools] industry. These institutions may have to implement a different set of policies than their peers located in the English-speaking world, which might result in additional investments on their part.
>
> *p. 834*

So, according to this argument, business schools in English-speaking countries are publishing far more than business schools in other countries and, if other countries want to catch up, they need to spend money. Although business schools might be an extreme case, the same principle no doubt applies in other disciplines. We might also point out, however, that, in a globalised academy, business schools in Anglophone countries would also likely have EAL scholars among their faculty members. This fact weakens Ryazanova, McNamara, and Aguinis's (2017) point somewhat, although it does not negate it.

Staying within the field of business, international collaboration has been shown to increase research and publication productivity, and very often countries will choose to collaborate with English-speaking countries because of the language factor. On the basis of another bibliometric study, this time based on authors' academic origin and university affiliation in the European nations, Aïssaoui, Geringer, and Livanis (2021) demonstrated how an internationalisation process of international business research has taken place over a period of time, driven by international collaboration strongly motivated by the English-language factor. On the basis of their findings, Aïssaoui, Geringer, and Livanis (2021) conclude that:

> while economic resources are central, they are not sufficient to support a nation's research productivity and global visibility. Instead, English proficiency stands as a critical resource which, when lacking, may further aggravate this [resource dependency] economic disadvantage. While European nations' reliance on the U.S. has decreased substantially, it has often been replaced by increasing reliance on the U.K. In addition, out of the 18 leading European authors, 12 were trained in either the U.K. or the U.S. In fact, the criticality

of English proficiency probably partly explains the U.K.'s emergence as the epicenter of IB [International Business] research in Europe.

p. 862

The desire to collaborate with Anglophones may thus be motivated by a need to access necessary levels of English-language proficiency. This fits in with Ammon's (2007) observation that Anglophones are likely to be able to produce "linguistically more refined texts" with "superior impact on the recipients" (pp. 124–125) and that they may be more mobile internationally and derive economic benefits through having English as their first language.

Flowerdew (2008) and La Madeleine (2007) refer to the emotional burden of having to perform and be evaluated in a second or foreign language. The following vignette from La Madeleine (2007) illustrates some of the stresses well:

> The nervous Japanese postdoc spent two weeks creating slides, 30 hours drafting a script and 44 hours rehearsing. Altogether, she spent one month away from the bench so that she would not disappoint her supervisors and colleagues during a short informal presentation, in English, before co-workers. Yet they remembered only the mistakes, she says.
>
> *p. 454*

An additional burden placed on the EAL scholar may be the need to write and publish in both English and their national language, to create two distinct but overlapping academic identities. This predicament is highlighted in studies by Casanave (1998) of Japanese scholars and by Shi (2003) of Chinese scholars who have returned to their home countries after graduate study in the US.

The issue of linguistic injustice in ERPP has been addressed in a number of surveys. In one such investigation, focused on nearly 600 Hong Kong Chinese scholars, Flowerdew (1999a) found that just over two-thirds of respondents thought themselves to be at a disadvantage as compared to Anglophones in terms of publishing an article in English. Similarly, almost 80% of the 154 mainland Chinese doctoral researchers in Li's (2002) survey felt disadvantaged as compared to Anglophones. Ferguson, Pérez-Llantada, and Plo (2011) obtained a similar result among a group of 300 Spanish scholars, finding, in addition, that self-reported English-language proficiency was a significant determinant of attitudes, that is, the weaker respondents felt their English to be, the less confidence they had in writing and publishing in English. In a smaller-scale survey of 91 Romanian economics academics, Muresan and Pérez-Llantada (2014) found that almost half of the subjects felt the dominance of English gave an unfair advantage to Anglophones. Addressing the issue in a different way, Hanauer, Sheridan, and Englander (2019) asked 148 Mexican and 236 Taiwanese researchers to rank the level of difficulty, satisfaction, and anxiety they experienced in science writing in English and their L1. Results revealed an average increase of 24% in difficulty, 10% in dissatisfaction, and 22% in anxiety for English. Ramirez-Castaneda (2020) surveyed 49 Colombian academics. According to the report, Colombia has one of the lowest levels of English proficiency in the world and yet 90% of scientific articles published by Colombian researchers are in English. The findings indicate that publishing in English creates additional financial costs to Colombian doctoral students and results in problems with reading comprehension, writing ease and time, and anxiety. Article rejection rates due to problems with language were reported as being high, as were decisions not to attend international conferences and meetings due to the mandatory use of English in oral presentations. The study also reviewed the cost of translation/editing services, with the cost per article estimated to be between a quarter and a half of a doctoral monthly salary in Colombia. Meanwhile, both Hewings, Lillis, and Vladimirou (2010) and Breeze (2015) have shown that EAL writers may be reluctant to cite publications which are not in English, even if they are written by colleagues in the same department, further demonstrating the advantage of English over other languages.

A counter-discourse on EAL inequality

In spite of the above findings regarding EAL inequality, a counter-discourse has developed that has questioned the value of making "binary 'native-non-native' distinctions" in academic publishing (Shvidko & Atkinson, 2019, p. 157). Swales (2004), an early proponent of this discourse, maintains that "the difficulties typically experienced by NNES academics in writing English are (certain mechanics such as article usage aside) *au fond* pretty similar to those experienced by native speakers" (p. 52). He argues that distinctions between experienced and novice scholars are more important. In a provocative paper, Hyland (2016) has more recently argued that linguistic disadvantage is a myth, that "academic English is no one's first language" and that it requires "deliberate learning" by both EAL writers and Anglophones (p. 57). Flowerdew (2019) and Politzer-Ahles, Holliday, Girolamo, Spychalska, and Harper Berkson (2017) point out, however, in strong rebuttals to Hyland, that while the latter point may be true, acquiring academic English in one's first language and in one's second or third language is not the same. As Flowerdew (2019) argues, EAL writers need more time and conscious learning to master what L1 writers develop as part of their upbringing and school education. That is not to say that novice Anglophone scholars do not also need help in accessing the international publication world, of course. They certainly encounter similar non-discursive issues to those of their EAL counterparts. Furthermore, some studies have found that Anglophone novice scholars have difficulty with syntax and academic vocabulary (Fazel, 2019; Habibie, 2016). Indeed, it is the case that the focus of the literature on EAL scholars may have had the unintended consequence of creating the impression that Anglophones do not experience difficulties when it comes to writing for publication and have a "free ride", to use Van Parijs's (2007) term, a phenomenon that Habibie (2019) has referred to as the *Lucky Anglophone Scholar Doctrine*:

> Thriving on native vs. non-native bipolarity, the discourse of the "*Lucky Anglophone Scholar*" doctrine projects a utopian image of the so-called Inner

Circle (Kachru, 1985) in which Anglophone scholars constitute a geo-linguistically homogenous population who participate in the construction and dissemination of scholarship naturally and willingly as a result of their native speaker status and/or membership in prestigious, well-resourced institutions of higher education.

p. 39

Another point to bear in mind is that there are, of course, many successful, highly published EAL scholars. Indeed, EAL scholars outnumber Anglophones worldwide. The term EAL writer (or speaker) is not precise, either; it covers a broad range of levels of competence (Flowerdew, 2019). Salager-Meyer (2008) distinguishes between those who have spent time in an English-speaking country or who belong to prestigious international research groups or laboratories in their home country and those who have never had the opportunity to spend time abroad. One might also distinguish between those who have had an English-speaking nanny (not at all an uncommon arrangement in many peripheral countries) and/or been educated in an international school/university and those who have not. Finally, it is worth bearing in mind that for many scholars, although English is not their mother tongue, it is nevertheless their first language as far as their professional literacy practices are concerned (Flowerdew, 2013a).

Certainly, as already indicated, there are non-discursive structures of inequality in academic publishing. Many contributors to the collection edited by Habibie and Hyland (2019) emphasise that EAL status is not the most significant difficulty for novice academics and that more challenging are issues shared with their Anglophone counterparts, such as familiarity with journal procedures, critical thinking skills, and competence in the academic register. Hultgren (2019), while not denying linguistic inequality, argues that more significant problems are "the resources and networks" available to scholars (p. 2). She provides data to show that only ten countries produce well over half of the world's total academic output, with the remainder shared among the 221 others. Data she provides also shows there to be a correlation between scientific output and GDP. The richer a nation, the more it publishes. Or, perhaps more pertinently, the poorer a country, the less it publishes. Swales (2004) also sees being "off-network" as a greater impediment to scholarly success than language, as does Belcher (2007), who finds authorial persistence and a willingness to revise and resubmit manuscripts to be an important key to success.

Furthermore, just because EAL scholars may feel disadvantaged because of a language gap, this does not mean that they do not see the value of publishing in English. For example, in Muresan and Pérez-Llantada's (2014) study cited above, although nearly half of the EAL participants felt at a disadvantage in having to use English, 63% considered themselves to be more advantaged than disadvantaged by using English in academic communication. Similar ambivalence was found in a study by Tardy (2004) among overseas, mostly East Asian, graduate students in a US university, who valued English as an international language of science, but at the same time, saw disadvantages for EAL scholars. The main reason EAL writers want to publish in English, as reported in various surveys, is to gain international exposure for their work (Martín, Rey-Rocha, Burgess, & Moreno, 2014; McDowell & Liardét, 2019; Shchemeleva, 2021; Stockemer & Wigginton, 2019).

World Englishes and English as a Lingua Franca

A final issue to consider with regard to English as a Global Language and ERPP is the actual variety (or varieties) of English that is used. World Englishes (WE) theory has been developed within the context of Kachru's concept of three "circles" of English (Kachru, 1985, 1992; Kachru, Kachru, & Nelson, 2006/2009). Kachru's theory divides the use of English in the world into three circles. The "Inner Circle" consists of nations such as the United Kingdom, the United States, and Australia, where English is the official first language. The "Outer Circle" is made up of former colonial countries such as India, Singapore, and Nigeria, where English is a second or official language. The "Expanding Circle" comprises countries in which English is a foreign language and is used also as an instrumental language in education, business, and other areas. Research into WE has highlighted the range of national and regional varieties of English around the globe and how different varieties of English are used in different countries and regions (Kachru, Kachru, & Nelson, 2006/2009; Kirkpatrick, 2010).

English as a Lingua Franca (ELF) theory is concerned with how English is used when EAL speakers and writers, from wherever they originate, communicate with each other in English (Jenkins, Baker, & Dewey, 2018). It has different, variable features from Standard British or American English. While WE theory is concerned with the legitimacy of locally established English varieties in the Outer Circle, ELF is more interested in English communication across geographical and cultural boundaries. These new varieties of English tend to be used in the spoken rather than the written research genres (Jenkins, 2011). They are very evident at international conferences and seminars and in university teaching, (Jenkins, 2011; Mauranen, Hynninen, & Ranta, 2010).

In spite of the new varieties of English (WE and ELF), the default variety of English for academic journals is "Standard" British or American English (some journals require "good" English, without defining it). Most journals state in their contributor guidelines that such a variety is required, many recommending that "non-native speakers" have their articles proofread by a "native speaker" prior to submission, a rather demeaning requirement for "non-native speakers" who are highly proficient in written academic English (Flowerdew, 2013a). For this reason, indeed, many linguists have for long rejected the native-speaker/non-native speaker dichotomy (Davies, 2006).

Journal policies notwithstanding, however, there are signs that some journals are allowing features of WE or ELF to be accepted or to slip through. Rozycki and Johnson (2013) conducted a corpus analysis of articles from the top engineering journals which had all been awarded a best-article-of-the year prize. Their

study showed the presence of lingua franca grammar, including non-standard article usage and a lack of concord in number marking between subject and predi-
cate, common issues familiar to teachers of ERPP. Rozycki and Johnson (2013)
claim that this is a sign that the majority of editors and reviewers in the field are
now "non-native" speakers of English. In a related corpus-based study, this time in
food science journals, Martinez (2018) created two parallel corpora, one authored
by EAL and the other by Anglophone writers, and found there to be a range of
lexical items used by EAL writers which were used much less or not at all by
Anglophone writers. For example, *besides* is frequently used by EAL writers as
a discourse marker equivalent to *thus* or *therefore*, where Anglophones prefer the
latter terms. Similarly, *nowadays* appears frequently in the EAL corpus, but is hardly
used at all in its Anglophone counterpart. Other items favoured by EAL writers
are *researches* and *works* used as plural count nouns, whereas their non-count forms
research and *work* are employed by Anglophones in the corpus. Focusing on two
time periods (2000–2005 and 2010–2015), Martinez also found this tendency to be
increasing over time. In a study of abstracts published by the journal *Social Science
Research*, Lorés-Sanz (2016) found that in 45% of the cases in her corpus of EAL
contributions to the journal, EAL writers rejected the canonical generic structure,
making it simpler, but with a higher degree of textual complexity. On the basis of
these findings, Lorés-Sanz argued that EAL writers may be contributing to the "(re)
shaping of written academic English at the level of rhetorics and textual organization" (p. 74) and that these alternative structures may be approved of (or overlooked
by) gatekeepers.

So, there is starting to be evidence that, on the syntactic, lexical, and rhet-
orical/organisational levels, EAL writers are beginning to make their presence felt.
Certainly, there have been suggestions that professional communities should have
a say in what is acceptable English rather than blindly following the "Standard
English" norms (Hynninen & Kuteeva, 2017; Wood, 2001). Gnutzmann and Rabe's
(2014) interview study conducted with German mechanical engineers seems to
suggest that when EAL scholars are in control of what is acceptable English or not,
they are able to deviate from the standard norms. On the other hand, Hynninen's
(2020) study of interventions in the text production processes by various mediators,
or *literacy brokers* (Lillis & Curry, 2010) and co-authors in Sweden during the
writing and evaluation processes of RAs in human–computer interaction and in
history revealed a more conservative approach, with authors and brokers having "a
strong incentive ... to follow Standard English correctness norms" (p. 20). Further
research is obviously needed in this area, not least because this issue has important
repercussions on what model of English to teach on courses and in workshops
on ERPP.

Conclusion

In this chapter, we have examined some of the discourses, discussions, and
perspectives with regard to English as a Global Language and their implications for

ERPP scholarship. We have considered two important, yet contrasting, discourses on the emergence, spread, and status of English: *laissez-faire* liberalism and linguistic imperialism. We have argued that a middle ground between these two poles needs to be found. We have also considered domain loss and the fact that the spread and dominance of English as a medium of academic discourse can pose a threat to the academic genres of other languages whose penetration in academic domains is decreasing. Focusing on how the contrasting discourses on English have been reflected in ERPP studies, we have concentrated on the debate concerning linguistic inequality, or injustice, with regard to EAL scholars. One of the contested topics in ERPP scholarship concerns the discourse that the current status and position of English as the lingua franca of academic discourse disadvantages EAL scholars, impeding them in their role in the construction and dissemination of knowledge and participation in global scholarship. We have also presented an emerging counter-discourse on this topic that has developed around the predicaments of Anglophone scholars, especially novice academics, in scholarly publication. Finally, we have discussed the place and implications of WE and ELF perspectives in ERPP studies and scholarship, showing how these varieties of English may gradually be making their way into ERPP and academic publication research.

5

THEORETICAL ORIENTATIONS IN ERPP

Introduction

Having considered some of the discourses and perspectives on English as a Global Language in the previous chapter, we will now look at some other common theoretical orientations that have framed and informed research within ERPP. Starting with genre theory, we will discuss the concept of genre and its development in applied linguistics and how this concept has been adopted to frame an understanding of the discursive practices of a discourse community. We will look at different constituent components of genre knowledge and the implications of this pivotal sociolinguistic concept for ERPP scholarship and scientific inquiry in this domain. Next, under the heading of social constructivist theory, we will examine two separate but related approaches within this overall paradigm: academic literacies and situated learning. We will explain how these frameworks view learning in general and literacy (writing) development in particular within a broader socio-contextual framework and how they have informed ERPP research. We will also briefly examine some key theoretical concepts that are common to both of these social constructivist approaches to literacy development: identity, power, and agency. Finally, we will consider World Systems Theory (mentioned in Chapter 2) as an influential theory that has played an important role in framing socio-economic differences and inequalities between the core and (semi)peripheral academic contexts and their positions in the current knowledge economy. As we discuss these theories and perspectives, we will highlight what they mean for ERPP and survey some ERPP studies that have applied them or been influenced by them.

DOI: 10.4324/9780429317798-5

Genre theory

Genre theory is concerned with how to define, categorise, and describe genres. The term genre in applied linguistics refers to "different communicative events which are associated with particular settings and which have recognised structures and communicative functions" (Flowerdew, 2013b, p. 139). Examples of genres are business reports, academic lectures, news articles, and recipes. Important genres in the context of ERPP, as mentioned in Chapter 1, would be research articles (RAs), editor's letters, referees' reports, conference presentations, academic blogs, book reviews, and research grant proposals. Genre refers not just to the organisation and lexico-grammatical properties of texts, but also the forms of cultural knowledge and understanding which lie behind them (Bawarshi & Reiff, 2010). Genre analysis, the application of genre theory, reveals how social purposes are expressed by formal features in texts, on the one hand, and how formal features in texts are employed to express social purposes, on the other (Bawarshi & Reiff, 2010).

Professional genres are usually specific to particular discourse communities (DCs), "groups that have goals or purposes, and use communication to achieve these goals" (Swales, 1990, p. 87). Obviously, there is a specific set of genres – most notably the research article (RA), but also the other genres referred to above – which belongs to the academic community. The concept of DC has framed a great deal of research into scholarly publication practices and experiences of scholars internationally (for early studies see Berkenkotter & Huckin, 1995; Bizzell, 1992; Swales, 1990). Practices of discourse communities act as screening mechanisms to include or exclude those who intend to join them. From this theoretical perspective, scholarly publication can be seen as a means of initiation, socialisation, and participation into the generic practices of one's disciplinary community. Therefore, one's participation and contribution to a DC in the form of scholarly publication hinges upon one's understanding of and allegiance to the community's socially constructed generic norms, and conventions. Berkenkotter and Huckin (1995) highlight the role of genres in DCs as follows:

> Genres are the media through which scholars and scientists communicate with their peers. Genres are intimately linked to a discipline's methodology, and they package information in ways that conform to a discipline's norms, values, and ideology. Understanding the genres of written communication in one's field is, therefore, essential to professional success.
>
> *p. 1*

In ERPP-related studies the concept of genre has provided an analytical lens through which to explore discursive and generic challenges and problems that EAL scholars or novice and doctoral researchers encounter in their writing for scholarly publication (e.g., Curry & Lillis, 2004; Flowerdew, 2000; Habibie, 2015, 2016; Li, 2006b; Liu, 2004).

Individual genres may be identified in terms of their communicative purposes (e.g., Swales, 1990). The (ostensive) purpose of the RA genre is the transmission of scientific knowledge, of the editor's letter to convey a decision regarding the publishability (or otherwise) of a submitted manuscript, and of a referee's report to provide an evaluation as to the publishability of a manuscript. This is rather simplistic, however, not least because, as Bhatia (1993) has noted, writers may have "private intentions" in addition to more transparent socially recognised communicative purposes. A scholar may seek to publish an article not only to convey scientific knowledge, but also, perhaps, to attack another scholar with whom they disagree. In addition, genres are staged, that is to say, they follow a specific sequential structure – for the RA, as we have seen, the typical structure is IMRaD – and each of these stages will have its own communicative purposes. For this reason, the different parts of the RA are often referred to as sub- or part-genres. And even within these sub-parts, there are communicative steps, which are again representative of separate purposes. A final distinctive feature of genres is that they exhibit characteristic lexico-grammatical patterns.

All the above features that we have set out have a degree of flexibility and there is thus room for individual creativity in genre production (Paltridge, 2012). Some genres are more conventionalised, however, than others; marriage oaths, for example, are very predictable and there is little, if any, room for divergence. The RA is also rather conventionalised, particularly if it is in the natural science disciplines and follows the IMRaD structure. Some have argued that for that reason it is easier to write an RA in the natural sciences than in the humanities, where the forms are much more diverse and require more individual creativity (Bazerman, 1988). Demonstrating this point, Gnutzmann and Rabe (2014) showed how biology scholars in a study they conducted employed "language re-use" writing strategies (Flowerdew & Li, 2007), copying chunks of language from other sources (to make sure that they complied with the generic norms), whereas history scholars displayed no evidence of such a practice and exhibited much more individuality and variation in how they wrote and structured the RA genre.

Because of its conventionalised nature, the various distinctive features of genres mean that they are amenable to pedagogic exploitation (Cheng, 2018). Systematic descriptions of the distinguishing features of genres, of how they are produced and how they are received, provide targets for learning. Similarly, novice scholars can be taught to operate as discourse analysts themselves and analyse target genres to inform their own writing. Indeed, studies have shown the use of "textual mentors" (Flowerdew & Wang, 2017), the reading of texts from the target genres with a view to imitation, to be a common writing strategy of novice scholars (Cheung, 2010; Okamura, 2006). Some writers take this too far, in fact, and, as reported by Flowerdew and Li (2007), use language re-use strategies and "copy and paste" quite large sections of text from published articles into their own texts and in doing so risk committing plagiarism. Furthermore, ERPP teachers (and researchers) can use the tools of genre analysis to analyse novice scholars' text production, with a view to identifying their strengths and weaknesses. In first-language contexts, some genres are acquired naturally in the home, but many have to be taught through the formal education system. In second language situations, especially those where there is little or no exposure to first-language contexts, all genres may need to be taught to a greater or lesser extent.

Tardy (2009) argues that genre knowledge is made up of a confluence of four dimensions: formal, process, rhetorical, and subject-matter genre knowledges.

- **Formal knowledge**: an understanding of the formal, structural, textual, discoursal, and lexico-grammatical aspects of genre; these features pose particular difficulties for, but are not confined to, EAL writers.
- **Process knowledge**: an understanding of the processes and procedures that are required to complete the communicative act; for example, planning, generating ideas, drafting, searching online for relevant literature.
- **Rhetorical knowledge**: an understanding of the intended purposes and persuasive dynamics within a rhetorical context; it is related to the writer's knowledge of their relationship with intended readers; it includes understanding background knowledge, hidden agendas, rhetorical appeals, surprise value, and Kairos (rhetorical timing), as they relate to the disciplinary community (Tardy, 2005); these are features of genre which are often occluded as far as the novice writer is concerned.
- **Epistemological knowledge** (also referred to as subject-matter knowledge): an understanding of the relevant scholarship and discipline-specific content; this type of knowledge is not a concern of ERPP per se, but how it interacts with the other types of knowledge may well be; for example, particular types of subject knowledge may require a particular type of formal knowledge on how it is best structured and presented.

Tardy's framework is helpful in understanding the challenges that scholarly writers come up against. An early study by Gosden (1996), for example, resonates with various aspects of Tardy's model. Gosden conducted interviews with 16 Japanese doctoral science students, asking them to describe how they went about writing RAs and their perceived problems. One of their difficulties related to formal knowledge: problems with lexico-grammar. They reported trying to correct grammar and sentence structure as the most frequent task to deal with between the first and second drafts of an article and improving vocabulary as the highest priority for subsequent drafts. With regard to process knowledge, they described four different ways of drafting a paper: (a) write in Japanese and then translate to English; (b) write an outline in Japanese and then complete the draft in English; (c) make notes and then convert them into full sentences in English; and (d) write a complete draft in English without any of the preliminary stages described in (a)–(c). With regard to rhetorical knowledge, the Japanese scientists identified a number of difficulties, including failing to be critical of previous research, failing to provide a clear justification for their approach, and a lack of a sense of audience.

A more recent case study by Habibie (2016) of an Anglophone doctoral participant also highlighted various issues which can be related to the different types of genre knowledge. Although the participant in Habibie's study, Samantha (a pseudonym), perhaps surprisingly, also reported some lexico-grammatical issues (formal knowledge), she had greater difficulties with other aspects of Tardy's formal knowledge, difficulties in structuring the RA and its constituent sections (IMRaD), for example. She furthermore highlighted some issues with process knowledge, in so far as she had problems in identifying functional differences between the different IMRaD sections and framing and disaggregating them so that they did not get mixed up. One strategy she used to overcome this problem in the literature review was to use sub-headings to better organise the issues she wanted to cover. Her challenges with regard to rhetorical knowledge included how to tailor the introduction section to what she perceived to be the readership and gatekeepers of the particular journal she was targeting. With the literature review, the difficulty was in moving beyond the preliminary steps and relating the existing literature to the argument she was developing. Furthermore, in the literature review, while she knew she should be critical, she also felt that she was not qualified enough to challenge what others had said or done. Illustrating how epistemological knowledge interacts with other types of genre knowledge, Samantha emphasised how her growing knowledge of the disciplinary orientations in her subject area (epistemological knowledge) allowed her to be "far more specific about the claims [she was] making and why they [were] of interest to scholars" (p. 56) (rhetorical knowledge).

What the studies cited above show is that genre theory is valuable in both the analysis of scholarly writing and in finding out what writers find difficult. Speaking as an experienced journal editor, Paré (2010) argues that submissions from many novice scholars are easily identified, because they fail to comply with the rhetorical conventions of the RA: "[T]he submissions are reasonable facsimiles of student or school genres, but ineffective journal articles. They display knowledge … but fail to address an actual dialogue among working scholars" (p. 30), that is, Tardy's rhetorical knowledge.

Social constructivist theory

As indicated in Chapter 1, social constructivist theories are based on the assumption that learning primarily takes place in social and cultural settings rather than solely within the individual. We will consider two approaches to ERPP research which draw on social constructivist theories in this section: academic literacies and situated learning. They are two separate approaches which each has its own adherents and literatures. However, we are dealing with them together here, because they have much in common (Lea, 2015) and have been brought together in various ERPP studies.

Academic literacies

Academic literacies (AL) views language, and reading and writing in particular, as a social practice (Barton & Hamilton, 1998; Lillis & Scott, 2007). The plural form, "literacies", highlights a focus on literacy as a range of practices around reading and writing in specific contexts, as opposed to a single cognitive activity (Lea, 2015). According to this view, texts do not exist in isolation, but are produced as part and parcel of what people do, both as individuals and as part of social institutions. Text production will vary according to context, culture, and genre. This is where AL theory links up with genre theory, because, according to this perspective, writers are required to switch their ways of writing according to setting and genre (Lea & Street, 2006); writing an RA is not the same as writing a PhD thesis, or a cover letter to a journal editor, for example. A practice perspective, furthermore, allows reading and writing to be linked to the broader social structures within which they take place and to which they at the same time contribute: globalisation, neoliberalism, Global English, etc. (Lillis & Curry, 2010). The AL model views writing as intimately connected to issues of identity and power (Lea & Street, 2006); identity, because individuals change as their literacy experiences develop; and power, because writers are subject to various external influences in their writing practices, both institutional and global. Finally, because literacy is viewed as practice, it allows for a focus on *literacy mediation* (Lillis & Curry, 2010), which in writing for publication may involve *literacy brokers* (various agents involved in the publication process – friends, colleagues, proofreaders, authors' editors, etc.) and *networks* (local or international groups contributing to and cooperating in the writing for publication process) (Burrough-Boenisch, 2003; Lillis & Curry, 2010; Li & Flowerdew, 2007; Luo & Hyland, 2021).

Situated learning

Given that much of the focus of ERPP is focused on novice scholars and what is required in order to become a fully-fledged expert in writing for publication (Flowerdew, 1999a, 1999b; Flowerdew, 2000; Mu, 2020), theories of learning become important and, given that writing for publication is not usually taught, but learned through practice, situated learning (SL) theory has been much adopted as an approach to ERPP research. It is an apprenticeship theory based on the assumption that learning occurs as part of being situated in a community. Learners start out on the periphery and through participation and practice gradually work their way to becoming fully-fledged members, in a process termed by Lave and Wenger (1991) as legitimate peripheral participation (LPP). This is where SL theory and discourse communities as part of genre theory overlap, as both see learning in terms of initiation into communities; genre theory, incidentally, is also a social constructivist and socially situated theory, although we have treated it separately.

LPP is a theoretical notion that has framed many studies in ERPP research (Casanave, 1998; Cho, 2004; Flowerdew, 2000, Habibie, 2016; Hasrati, 2005; Li, 2005, 2006b, 2007a, 2014a; Shi, 2003; Tardy, 2005). From this theoretical perspective, scholarly publication is a means of initiation, socialisation, and participation in the practices of one's community of practice. The term Community of Practice (CoP) (Lave & Wenger, 1991) is similar to Discourse Community (DC) (Swales, 1990). They both refer to the practices, purposes, ideologies, learning practices, and rituals of groups of people, but DC puts more emphasis on language and communication than does CoP. LPP is both a learning and membership act and process whereby geographically, linguistically, and experientially, peripheral members of academic communities (including doctoral students, novice and EAL academics) join those communities and develop the required literacies through engagement and under supervision of more experienced members of their CoP/DC. Novices can be considered as members of CoPs, but their participation is initially marginal and limited. The theoretical notion of LPP has served as an analytical lens to explore the challenges that scholars, especially EAL and novice scholars, face in joining and participating in the practices of their academic communities, novice–expert relationships such as graduate student–supervisor relationships, and literacy development within and beyond academic contexts.

Important notions common to both academic literacies and situated learning identity

Considering writing for publication as a process of socialisation or enculturation into DCs/CoPs brings into play issues of identity, power, and agency (Duff, 2010; Flowerdew & Wang, 2015; Paltridge, 2015). As we saw in Chapters 2 and 3, publication in international refereed journals acts as a benchmark of scholarly achievement. The development of the ability to achieve such publication can be construed of as a process of identity construction, as a passage from novice to expert, from exclusion to acceptance as a bona fide member of the academic disciplinary community (Casanave & Vandrick, 2003). In this reading, identity is not a fixed attribute, but is discursively and dynamically constructed through interaction with DCs/CoPs. As documented in many studies (Curry & Lillis, 2013; Flowerdew, 2000; Li, 2006a, 2006b, 2007a, 2014a, 2014b; Mur-Dueñas, 2019), this process of identity development can be highly problematic, both in a practical sense – in developing the ability to write an appropriate text in accordance with the generic requirements of the target journal and negotiate with the various gatekeepers (editors and reviewers) to get it published – and psychologically – in overcoming the emotional barriers which dealing with such practical difficulties brings with it. Criticism and rejection are inevitable features of the publication process and they need to be expected and dealt with (Kwan, 2013), as has again been shown in various studies (Flowerdew, 2000; Li, 2006a).

Power and agency

Viewing academic socialisation as identity formation requires a consideration of power. Academic socialisation requires social interaction – with peers, with colleagues, with mentors, with gatekeepers, and with others – and all of these interactions are affected by power relations. The novice scholar is typically in a weak position vis-à-vis these other interactants and, as access to the discourse community is negotiated, power is gradually acquired. Li's (2006b) "sociopolitically-oriented" case study focused on a Chinese doctoral science student, for example, showed how "power-infused" relationships with the participant's institutional context, his supervisors (who had greater expertise and authority), and the gatekeepers of his target journals affected his writing process. In Huang's (2010) study of 11 Taiwanese doctoral students, the students depended on their supervisors for funds and equipment; they felt as if they were employees rather than students, but the supervisors were listed as corresponding authors. Due to this differential power relation, the students lost motivation to learn. Power differentials operate at a more macro level also. Typically, EAL scholars and scholars in the periphery countries (see below) are in weaker positions than Anglophone scholars and scholars in the centre, respectively (Lillis & Curry, 2010) when it comes to writing and getting work published.

Power is not an immutable force, however, and individual agency can do much to counteract it. As Duff (2010, p. 171) puts it, "[t]hose being socialized have agency and powers of resistance, innovation, and self-determination and are not likely to simply reproduce or internalize the complete repertoire of linguistic and ideological resources in their midst". Thus, the novice writer in Li's (2006b) study was willing to go through six rounds of "revise and resubmit" and even made an appeal to the divisional associate editor of the journal before his article was finally accepted. In a more congenial setting, Darvin and Norton (2019) describe how a supervisor and doctoral student were able to reconfigure the traditional hierarchical power relationship and construct a third space, where "identities are in a state of flux where novice and expert become peers, and where established scholars interrupt their privileged status" (p. 192).

World Systems Theory

One of the theories that has influenced and informed ERPP scholarship and research to a great extent is Wallerstein's World Systems Theory (briefly referred to already in previous chapters). Wallerstein (1974, 2004) developed this theory to account for the inner workings of the world in terms of international relations and politics at a global macro scale. The theory divides the world into three macrospheres: core countries, semi-periphery countries, and periphery countries. It analyses interstate relationships and power dynamics from an economic perspective according to the division of labour. Each sphere also comprises its own core and periphery. The economies of the core countries, the advanced Western countries (the US and the advanced countries of Western Europe), are high-skilled economies, while those of the periphery countries (e.g., Bangladesh, Bolivia, Cambodia, Egypt, Sri Lanka) are based on the production of raw materials. Semi-peripheral states (e.g., countries of the former Soviet Union, Portugal, Spain) are intermediate between the core and periphery. They act as a buffer between core and periphery and may include declining core or rising periphery countries. The model is not static and states within each sphere ascend or descend to a higher or lower stratum. The hegemony of the core is sustained through its economic power and the raw materials it exploits from the periphery and the (semi)periphery's dependence on it for support and expertise. That is, in this one-sided asymmetrical relationship, the core tends to keep getting richer and the (semi)periphery gets poorer; it is thus difficult, although not impossible, to move up the scale (e.g., China and some South East Asian states are rising in status).

ERPP scholarship has adapted this theory to analyse the geopolitics of the construction and dissemination of knowledge. The adapted theory can be used to explore asymmetries in academic contexts in terms of access and availability of scientific and cultural resources and systems of power in the establishment and legitimisation of knowledge, what Foucault (1980) refers to as "regimes of thought" or "regimes of truth". From this ERPP perspective, the core is smaller than in the mainstream economic theory and the English language is one of the key criteria in characterising that sphere. The core is thus made up of those economically strong countries in which English is the dominant language, including the US, Canada, the UK, Australia, and New Zealand. The periphery and semi-periphery are the non-Anglophone/EAL periphery countries. Just like its economic counterpart, in this model, the relationship between these spheres is asymmetrical and exploitative. Thanks to its economic and political power, the Anglophone core is the key player in cultural politics at the global level, where it extends its linguistic imperialism (Phillipson, 1992) and sustains its academic and linguistic hegemony, in order to dominate the EAL periphery and semi-periphery. It sets the rules of the academic game, including scholarly publication, and makes others play by those rules. Not only does it impose its language (English) on the periphery and monopolise the medium of academic discourse, but it also determines and legitimates its preferred discourses, methodologies, practices, and ideologies.

A close look at the scholarship and research within ERPP does show the significance of the key concepts of core and periphery and how this dichotomised perspective has framed the analytical lens of ERPP. ERPP research has considered how the division of labour and linguistic and economic (and to some extent political) inequalities, asymmetries, and differences between the core and periphery have disadvantaged peripheral and semi-peripheral EAL scholars (or advantaged Anglophone scholars) in the construction, adjudication, certification, and dissemination of knowledge. An influential study that has used this model to bring to the fore discursive (linguistic) and non-discursive (non-linguistic) asymmetries and challenges between the core and the periphery is Canagarajah's (2002) *A geopolitics of academic writing*, which compared his (and his colleagues') scholarly publication practices and experiences in the context of the US and war-torn Sri Lanka. Based on his experience as a scholar in both Sri Lanka and the US, Canagarajah (2002) emphasised the role of non-discursive issues in limiting the participation of peripheral EAL scholars in global scholarship. Non-linguistic and material issues, such as availability and access to photocopying, stationery, postal services, electricity, computers, and state-of-the-art literature play an equally important role in limiting peripheral participation as discursive impediments created by the need to conduct research and publication in English, he argued.

Critiquing Canagarajah's (2002) core vs. periphery dichotomy, however, Bennett (2015) argues that apart from core and peripheral countries, there are countries (in Southern and Eastern Europe in Bennett's case: Portugal, Italy, Greece, Spain, Croatia, Serbia, Czech Republic, Romania, Poland, and Turkey) that "fall between the two camps, being neither in the 'premier league' nor properly of the 'third world'" (p. 156). Although the academic landscape in this zone does not comprise completely "meritocratic institutions", it is not a case of what Canagarajah calls "minifiefdoms" dominated by nepotism and personal connections either. Bennett (2015) uses the term *Butler Syndrome* to characterise the status and role of the semi-peripheral countries in global socio-political as well as academic dynamics.

> Like the butler in a stately home that emulates his master and despises members of his own class, semi-peripheral scholars and institutions may become more precious about centre values than the core countries themselves, leading them to reject markers of their own identity in favour of imported ones that are perceived to carry more status.
>
> *p. 157*

The ever-increasing pressure on the semi-peripheral academics to publish their work in high-impact English-medium international journals, as well as English-medium, in preference to mother tongue, instruction in many semi-peripheral academic contexts, is indicative of this tendency for emulation. At the same time, semi-peripheral institutions may act as hubs of subsidiary networks, crossing the language barrier between English and local languages. Knowledge published in English may be disseminated to the subsidiaries in the local language and knowledge created in the local language may be uploaded in English via the hub. Bennett illustrates this process between Spain and its former Latin American colonies. Because of this brokering role, the semi-periphery may be criticised as being imitative and lacking in originality (Bennett, 2015). We would note that these tendencies are more noticeable in the HSS disciplines than in the natural sciences.

On this theme, on the basis of a quantitative survey of Brazilian scholars (N = 290), Monteiro and Hirano (2020) take another tack on the semi-periphery, identifying a periphery within a (semi-)periphery, insofar as international publication has been adopted in the hard sciences but the humanities and social sciences have been left on the periphery, that is, not taking up publication in English. This is a disciplinary distinction which has been noted in other jurisdictions (Li, & Flowerdew, 2009; López-Navarro, Moreno, Quintanilla, & Rey-Rocha, 2015; Petric, 2014; Uysal, 2014).

Overall, there is no doubt that the core vs. (semi)periphery conceptualisation and discourse can play a significant role in providing a master narrative about how the academic world works and the structures and orders that dominate its inner workings. However, as Appadurai (1990) argues, the problem with Wallerstein's model (and other Marxist theories of global development) is that it overlooks "disorganized capitalism" (Lash & Urry, 1987) and disjunctures between economy, culture, and politics. That is, "[t]he new, global, cultural economy has to be understood as a complex, overlapping, disjunctive order, which cannot any longer be understood in terms of existing center-periphery models (even those that might account for multiple centers and peripheries)" (Appadurai, 1990, p. 296). This view provides a more dynamic perspective of the world system, where disjunctures are now an inherent characteristic of the politics of global culture and where "people, machinery, money, images, and ideas now follow increasingly nonisomorphic paths" (Appadurai, 1996, p. 37). The increasing influence of universities in countries in Asia is a good example of this phenomenon.

Conclusion

In this chapter, we have considered a number of common theoretical and conceptual orientations adopted by ERPP scholars: genre theory, social constructivist theory, and World Systems Theory. First, we have explained how the conceptual lens of genre theory has framed an understanding of discursive and generic challenges and problems that academics, especially peripheral and novice ones, face in their academic writing and scholarly publication practices. Subsequently, we considered two separate but related approaches to ERPP which draw on social constructivist theory: academic literacies and situated learning. Furthermore, we have examined key notions of identity, power, and agency that apply to both of these theoretical orientations. As we have seen, all of these theories have been drawn upon in ERPP research and practice. What all of these theories demonstrate is that novice scholarly writers need to develop specialist discipline-specific literacies and acquire a complex set of knowledge, competencies, and expertise and are subject to a whole range of competing socio-political and ideological forces and dynamics. Although they are legitimate members of their academic communities, their participation is limited and peripheral. It is only through engagement and once they have been through community practices and challenges that they can be accepted as full members of their chosen DCs/CoPs. Needless to say, it is incumbent on ERPP researchers to explore discursive and non-discursive challenges and struggles that scholars in different academic contexts encounter for scholarly publication and shed light on the true, complex nature of those challenges and problems. It is also the task of ERPP practitioners to develop appropriate remedial interventions and strategies and facilitate the socialisation and legitimate peripheral participation process of academics as best as they can.

6

RESEARCH APPROACHES IN ERPP

Introduction

Having considered theoretical issues (along with their applications to ERPP) in previous chapters, in this chapter, we will look at two empirical approaches to ERPP research: genre analysis and naturalistic studies. We have already discussed the theories behind these two approaches in the previous chapter, namely genre theory and social constructivist theory. Here, we will be focusing more on the empirical work that has been conducted within the framework of these two theories, although there might be some overlap. The two approaches to be focused upon in this chapter are not the only empirical approaches employed in ERPP studies – quantitative survey and interviews are other approaches, for example, as indicated in Chapter 1 – but they are probably the most frequently used and have yielded important applicable findings. As with the theoretical contexts in which they are situated (as seen in Chapter 5), the two approaches are related. Both of them investigate text in context, but genre analysis tends to focus more on the text end of the text–context continuum, while naturalistic approaches (also sometimes referred to as ethnographic or ethnographically oriented approaches) are more concerned with the practices that surround text. In making this generalisation, however, it should be borne in mind that either approach may be further away from or less close to either end of the continuum (Flowerdew, 2011). In terms of application, as already mentioned in the previous chapter, genre analysis provides descriptions which can provide models for analysing and understanding texts, on the one hand, and frameworks for creating texts on the other. Naturalistic approaches provide accounts of how scholars go about writing and how they deal with other stakeholders, such as co-authors, various literacy brokers, and gatekeepers. Such accounts reveal the perceptions, problems, and strategies that scholars are likely to come up against. They provide valuable exemplars that can be used as case studies

DOI: 10.4324/9780429317798-6

in ERPP courses and their findings may have implications for institutional policies, such as highlighting the need for ERPP training.

Genre analysis of research English

Although genre analysis is a very broad term, with regard to ERPP, we are usually concerned with the linguistic description of the texts and their surrounding contexts that go to make up the research genres, primarily the research article (RA), but also others we have mentioned in previous chapters. The goal of such descriptions is to gain insights into how meanings are expressed in the genres of research English in order to employ these insights in the teaching and learning process. Research has shown that academic texts are subject to systematic generic and disciplinary variations (Hyland, 2000/2004, 2012). That means that if these systematic features can be described, such descriptions can feed into writing pedagogy. The landmark publication in this domain is Swales's (1990) seminal study, *Genre analysis: English in academic and research setting.* The book provides a theoretical framework for the analysis of English as the language of research from a genre perspective, with practical applications, in particular, to the teaching and learning of research English.

Prior to Swales, there was a tradition in linguistic research into scientific text, known as register analysis, which involved the manual counting of frequencies of lexis and grammatical forms (e.g., Barber, 1962). Although this analysis was useful − it ascertained that the continuous tenses were extremely rare in scientific text, for example (and therefore, arguably, not deserving much attention in a scientific English course) − the analysis was purely formal, with little attention paid to meaning or textual and social context. Register analysis was followed by a more rhetorical period, where researchers began to consider the relation between language form and rhetorical functions in scientific text and how sentences and paragraphs were put together (see Benesch, 2001, for a summary). Swales took this work further, emphasising genre and how academics use the RA as a means of communication within their disciplinary discourse communities (DCs) (see Chapter 5 for a definition). In writing an RA, an academic is therefore engaged in a form of communication with their peers and performing a genre. Swales (1990, p. 58) defined genre as:

> a class of communicative events, the members of which share some set of communicative purposes. … In addition to purpose, exemplars of a genre exhibit various patterns of similarity in terms of structure, style, content and intended audience.

As well as shared audience, Swales thus identified a degree of systematicity and predictability in terms of the structure of genres. With regard to the RA, in his detailed analysis of a sample of their introduction sections, he identified that they followed a conventionalised pattern of rhetorical moves and steps, determined by the communicative purposes of the writers. The pattern of these moves he labelled the CARS (Create A Research Space) model, because moving through the series of communicative stages in the RA introduction builds an argument for the importance of one's study and opens up the space for the main body of the research. Thus, a writer highlights their contribution to the field by first identifying the field of enquiry and summarising previous research, second by identifying a gap in the existing work, and third, summarising how they will fill this gap. Figure 6.1 shows the model, referred to as the schematic structure, in more detail in terms of the three moves and supporting steps:

This simple pattern has had a tremendous effect on ERPP pedagogy, in providing a pattern for novice (and more experienced) writers to structure their introductions. In a later monograph, Swales (2004) extended his theory, emphasising that individual genres do not exist in isolation, but are intertextually related one to the other in families, hierarchies, sets, systems, and chains. For example, an RA does not exist in a vacuum, but is likely preceded by a conference presentation, which is itself preceded by an abstract, and which involves interaction and feedback with the audience; following the conference, a first draft will be submitted to a journal and (in the case of a successful paper) this will likely go through several rounds of review and revised versions before the final version is accepted. From a pedagogical perspective this is a useful insight, because it shows that the teaching and learning of the RA genre should not be considered in isolation from its other family members.

Move 1. Establishing a territory:
      Step 1. Claiming centrality
      and/or
      Step 2. Making topic generalisation
      and/or
      Step 3. Reviewing items of previous research
Move 2. Establishing a niche:
      Step 1A. Counterclaiming
      or
      Step 1B. Indicating a gap
      or
      Step 1C. Question-raising
      or
      Step 1D. Continuing a tradition
Move 3. Occupying the niche:
      Step 1A. Outlining purposes
      or
      Step 1B. Announcing present research
      Step 2. Announcing principal findings
      Step 3. Indicating research article structure

FIGURE 6.1 Schematic structure of research article introductions
Source: Adapted from Swales (1990)

It is very common for a conference presentation or a conference poster to be later turned into an RA and it makes sense to mimic this process pedagogically.

Since Swales's seminal work, many studies have been conducted into both the move structure and the conventionalised lexico-grammatical realisations of the typical moves of the different parts of the RA. Thus, for example, Lorés-Sanz (2004) and Stotesbury (2003) examined abstracts; Lu, Casal, and Liu, (2020) and Milagros del Saz Rubio (2011) have looked at introductions; Bruce (2009) and Williams (1999) have examined results; Cotos, Huffman, and Link (2017) have considered methods; and Basturkmen (2012) and Peacock (2002) have investigated the discussion section. Stoller and Robinson (2013) is a pedagogically oriented book-length study of the move structure of all of the sections in a corpus of chemistry articles, while Nwogu (1997) is an early paper analysing the move structure of all of the sections of the medical RA. Cotos, Huffman, and Link (2015) employ a corpus of RAs and validate cross-disciplinary move/step IMRaD frameworks. Some of these analyses can be extremely fine-grained; for example, Le and Harrington's (2015) study of word clusters used to comment on results in the discussion section of quantitative RAs in the field of applied linguistics, or Gillaerts and Van de Velde's (2010) study of interactional metadiscourse in RA abstracts, to take just two of many studies.

Much of the above-cited research focuses on particular disciplines and, indeed, disciplinary variation has been the target of much genre analysis conducted on the RA. This is important, because, as these studies have shown, all of the features analysed in the research cited above are likely to vary according to discipline. Lin and Evans (2012) (previously referred to in Chapter 3), for example, analysed the macro-structures of 433 empirical RAs from four disciplinary groupings in high-impact journals, finding disciplinary variation in the major generic structures of these articles.

Although corpus techniques had not come into their own at the time Swales was conducting his work on genre theory, much genre analysis since has used such techniques and they are employed in many of the above-cited studies. While the identification of rhetorical moves and steps is still problematic for corpus analysis (although see e.g., Cortes, 2013; Cotos, Huffman, & Link, 2015; Moreno & Swales, 2018), they allow for powerful automatic analysis of the lexico-grammatical features of genres. Intensive work has been done on such features as vocabulary, lexical bundles, stance markers, and metadiscourse (see references to the plethora of this work in Riazi, Ghanbar, & Fazel, 2020).

An important researcher who has used a corpus approach to look at the RA genre (along with other academic genres) using corpora is Hyland. Hyland's approach is more contextual, because, in addition to the corpus data, he interviews professional scholars who have written and work with such texts. In his *Disciplinary discourses: Social interactions in academic writing* (Hyland, 2000/2004), he uses a corpus made up of various academic genres across eight disciplines to investigate how various textual features are used in different ways across disciplines to express authors' intended meanings. In his later monograph, *Disciplinary identities: Individuality and community in academic discourse* (Hyland, 2012), again using a corpus of various academic genres and interviews with insiders, he turns his attention to the tension between author identity and disciplinary and institutional expectations, as conveyed by various textual features. Because he makes use of insider perspectives, Hyland is able to not only describe the various pragmatic features he is interested in, but can also explain and interpret them in the context of the broader communicative purposes they are designed to achieve. Thus, as well as producing findings that can be directly incorporated into teaching materials, Hyland's work provides valuable insights for the ERPP practitioner in how to understand the disciplinary values of their potential students.

Finally, we need to consider genre analysis conducted from a comparative intercultural rhetoric perspective (Connor, 2011). Studies have shown that different languages and cultures have their preferred ways of academic writing (McIntosh, Connor, & Gokpinar-Shelton, 2017) – in terms of rhetorical features, logical argument, and linguistic features. These differences may range from the tiniest pragmatic features, such as stance markers, to the highest level of discourse organisation, such as the macro-structure of the RA or grant proposal. Thus, at the micro-level, for example, Hu and Cao (2011) investigated how hedging and boosting varied in abstracts in English and Chinese RAs. At the organisational level, to take two other examples, Loi, Evans, Lim, and Akkakoson (2016) and Sheldon (2018) have shown respectively how discussion sections in Malay and conclusion sections in Spanish may be structured differently. A number of studies of the move structure of introductions to RAs in Malay (Ahmad, 1997), Thai (Jogthong, 2001), and Brazilian Portuguese (Hirano, 2009), respectively, have shown differences as compared to English. Awareness of such contrasts can be useful for plurilingual writers targeting international journals, allowing them to adjust their writing to the Anglo-American style. At the same time, as we said in Chapter 4, some ERPP scholars have argued that various cultural styles should be accepted by international journals, not just Anglophone models, and, as we saw again in Chapter 4, there is some evidence that this is starting to happen.

All of the descriptions reported in the above paragraphs offer useful insights into the intricacies of the relations between form and function in academic discourse, on the one hand, and input for a more linguistically oriented approach to ERPP pedagogy, on the other. It is worth noting some important gaps in research as far as ERPP is concerned, however. Very little is known about humanities RAs as compared to natural sciences disciplines, perhaps because their structures are much more variable. Other scholarly genres besides the RA are also relatively neglected. There is quite a lot of literature on conference presentations (Dubois, 1980a; Hood & Forey, 2005; Rowley-Jolivet & Carter-Thomas, 2005a, 2005b; Wulff, Swales, & Keller, 2009), including multimodal analysis (Dubois, 1980b; Morell, 2015; Rowley-Jolivet, 2002, 2012), and there is some material on book reviews (Motta-Roth, 1998; Salager-Meyer, 2010; Salager-Meyer, Alcaraz Ariza, & Pabón Berbesí, 2007; Salmani Nodoushan & Montazeran, 2012; Tse & Hyland, 2008). There is also a certain amount of published research on some of the occluded genres (referees' reports and editors' letters), although this tends to be on data from applied linguistics, which researchers (as editors and reviewers) have had access to. We will review that literature separately in Chapter 7, where we return to the theme of peer review. Finally, some research has been done on research grants, another occluded genre, although some organisations publish guidelines on how they want their proposals to be organised. Citing Berkenkotter and Huckin (1995) and Myers (1990), Feng and Shi (2004) describe the research grant proposal as "an initial step in the process of knowledge production" (p. 8). In genre analysis terms, it represents the first stage in a discourse chain that will end up, hopefully, in publications. A novice scholar working on a PhD may not consider research grants as an important genre (although they might have to apply for a small-scale university research grant for their study). However, once they are appointed to a tenure track position they may be encouraged, or increasingly required, to obtain research grants, grants and amount of funding being important indicators of research esteem. While most grant proposal formats are unique, it is nevertheless possible to identify some typical organisational macro-structures, rhetorical move patterns within those larger structures, and lexico-grammatical features within those move patterns (Khadka, 2014; Matzler, 2021). Descriptions of such exemplars provide useful potential models, therefore, for writing. Relevant studies are those of Connor (1998, 2000); Connor and Mauranen (1999); Connor and Upton (2004); Connor and Wagner (1999); Cotos (2019); Feng and Shi (2004); Khadka, (2014); Matzler, (2021); and Tseng (2011). Meanwhile, in a combined research and pedagogic approach, L. Flowerdew (2016) showed how she designed and implemented a writing module focusing on grant proposal abstracts for postgraduate students.

Naturalistic studies of research and publication processes

The naturalistic approach to ERPP investigation views language as more of a social practice than does the more textually oriented discourse analytic approach, although text is still at the heart of the enquiry. It uses ethnographic methods rather than detailed textual analysis and works with case studies. It investigates how individuals and groups go about writing for publication, including how they conduct their research, how they construct their texts, and how they interact with others (co-authors, editors, and various other literacy brokers, Lillis & Curry, 2010). In so doing, it highlights their perceptions, their problems, and their strategies, thereby providing lessons for others who are also interested in the ERPP endeavour, whether they be ERPP researchers, ERPP practitioners (who can draw on such accounts in their teaching), or scholars writing for publication themselves. We will first run though some of the tenets of the approach and then look at some of the studies conducted to date.

In terms of data, naturalistic approaches rely on interviews, observations, diaries, field notes, and relevant official documents and artefacts. Interviews may be life history interviews (Clandinin & Connelly, 2000), discourse-based interviews (Odell, Goswami, & Harrington, 1983) (more recently referred to as talk around text, Lillis,

2008), text-history interviews (Lillis & Curry, 2010), or some combination. Having data from a range of sources provides for triangulation and tests the validity of the research. Naturalistic enquiry in ERPP also often analyses research participants' texts (drafts and submitted versions) and editorial correspondence. Because trust needs to be built up with research participants, the research may be spread over a considerable time, even years. As well as allowing trust to develop with participants, such "prolonged engagement" (Lincoln & Guba, 1985) allows the research to build up an insider's (*emic*) perspective (Lillis, 2008; Paltridge, Starfield, & Tardy, 2016; Watson-Gegeo, 1988). Findings are not presented in terms of numbers, but more likely in the form of evocative vignettes and/or quotations from interviews in what is called a *thick description* (Geertz, 1983).

Theory in this type of research is often described as "grounded" (Bryant & Charmaz, 2019). That is to say, the researcher does not start with a theory they want to test, but instead constructs the theory from the ground up, from the data they collect, although they will of course be familiar with the literature and the situation at hand, and may draw on an existing theory as the analysis develops (Davis, 1994). The theory that emerges will not be a "grand" theory, but will be a system that allows for an understanding of participants and the situation under investigation. It will not be able to make claims to generalisability to other settings, although the researcher would be guided in their research to ask questions which might provide answers of value to ERPP research models, institutional policy, or teaching materials. Some case study research in ERPP is part of a larger research project and may also include quantitative data collected from surveys, for example.

The first study to use a naturalistic approach to enquiry in ERPP is St. John's (1987) investigations into the writing processes of a group of Spanish scientists writing for publication in English, a study we have referred to already in previous chapters. It is no coincidence that St. John was working in the university department of which Swales was the head at the time, at the University of Aston, UK. St. John began collecting the data for this study while she was teaching two ERPP courses at the University of Cordoba for science students. She collected the main body of the data 14 months later, however, when she interviewed a number of finance researchers, drawing on their published articles and drafts of papers in progress in order to investigate their problems and strategies as EAL writers. She also examined articles made available by the participants following the interviews, and studied published finance articles in both English and Spanish.

St. John's findings drew on an analysis of participants' texts, with some interpretation of their cognitive processes and motives, based on the interviews and informal discussions. She noted that few organisational changes were made once the initial drafts had been completed, a finding which she attributed to participants' prior exposure to many articles in English and a similar format for articles in both English and Spanish. 80–90% of changes were to do with word order and lexis. While some participants started to write first in Spanish and then translate or have their work translated into English, they soon changed to writing directly in English, which was the choice of all participants. Three strategies were used: writing directly in their own English; writing from a Spanish outline; or building a jigsaw using published articles as a source. All participants employed an Anglophone or highly competent English speaker to check and edit their texts. They found the discussion the most difficult section to write, followed by the introduction, with the method and results being the easiest. They tended to rely on adapting text from previous texts while writing.

We can see from this study that the naturalistic approach, supported by textual analysis, can yield interesting data on how a group of EAL writers go about writing for publication, along with their perceptions, problems, and strategies with regard to the issue. Although no generalisations can be made from the findings, they provide baseline data on which to compare subsequent findings in comparable situations.

We have previously cited the work of Canagarajah in the context of World Systems Theory (Chapter 5), which is one of the theories that he invokes in his partly autobiographical case study conducted while he was working as a scholar in Jaffna, Sri Lanka (Canagarajah, 1996, 2002). It is an account of the difficulties he and his colleagues experienced in conducting research and attempting international publication in a peripheral context at a time of civil war. His data consisted mostly of field notes based on participant observation and articles published by his academic colleagues (he was unable to conduct formal interviews because of the situation in Jaffna at the time) (Canagarajah, 2002). Non-discursive deficiencies identified by Canagarajah included disruption to the power supply, limited access to communication facilities, lack of library facilities and consequent difficulty in meeting the deadlines of centre journals, on the one hand, and, more fundamentally, in putting together a well-documented and adequately-referenced article in the first place, on the other. In spite of the challenges, Jaffna scholars had "coping strategies" (p. 466), such as making up for lack of reference material by strategic use of secondary sources and passing them off as based on primary sources and inserting references to works that had not been read. As mentioned, World Systems Theory and the centre/periphery dichotomy are drawn upon to explain Canagarajah's data, although Canagarajah is at pains to point out that he does not make any claims for other periphery contexts. Nevertheless, this naturalistic study provides data upon which to compare other periphery (and centre) settings where scholars are striving for international publication.

Flowerdew's (2000) single case study is of a young Hong Kong Chinese scholar who completed his doctoral studies in the US and returned to a position as a junior academic at a university in his home city. He was working towards tenure, a process which required international publications. The researcher and an assistant followed the participant over an extensive period, with data sources including the participant's draft and final texts; interviews and email communication with the participant; communications between the student and the journal editor, reviewers, and in-house editor; field notes; and discussion with an editor who helped the student with his writing. All these data reveal the editorial changes that were made to the article in order to bring it into line with the editorial leanings and style of the target journal, highlighting how an article is often the work of more actors in addition to the author(s). The study was part of a broader one involving a large-scale survey of Cantonese-mother-tongue scholars in Hong Kong (Flowerdew, 1999a), an in-depth interview study of a sample of these scholars (Flowerdew, 1999b), and an interview study with journal editors, seeking their views on contributions from Hong Kong scholars (Flowerdew, 2001).

Two theories were invoked to account for the data in this study: discourse community (Swales, 1990) and legitimate peripheral participation (Lave & Wenger, 1991) (see Chapter 5). It became clear as the study progressed that the participant was trying to gain access to the discourse community of scholars in his field, as represented by the editors and reviewers of the journals he was interacting with, who were acting as gatekeepers (and counsellors). The whole process of seeking publications was also a learning experience in which he had to learn for himself through engaging in the practice. The conclusion to the study was that the experience of the participant represented what it means to be a multilingual researcher seeking international publication in English.

Lillis and Curry's (2010) book-length investigation into the writing and publication practices of 50 multilingual psychology scholars in four periphery European countries is a seminal publication highlighting the potential of the naturalistic approach to researching ERPP. Data collected over several years included participants' manuscripts and drafts, interviews, observations, document analysis, analysis of written correspondence, and reviewers' and editors' comments. Lillis and Curry made use of what they refer to as "text histories", an approach previously used by Flowerdew (2000), but on a much larger scale by Lillis and Curry, involving the collection of the various drafts of a manuscript and data from as many people involved in the manuscript as possible (editors, reviewers, colleagues, etc.), including cyclical face-to-face discussion with authors of the manuscripts and drafts. The authors also made great use of ethnographic vignettes to illustrate the research and publication process.

One of the main findings of the study was that knowledge construction is not the product of a single author, but is a joint production involving many parties besides the author(s), referred to by Lillis and Curry as literacy brokers. Another key finding is that EAL scholars in the study rely on participation in both local and international networks in the writing and publication processes. Lillis and Curry also examine the hierarchical power relations between the two levels of "local" and "global". These levels are important when scholars decide where to publish their work; new, original research is targeted at international journals, while overviews and applied work are more likely targeted at local journals. A number of theories are drawn upon to interpret the data in this complex study, including World Systems Theory (Wallerstein, 2004), conceptions of competence and performance in language production (Hymes, 1974), and social network analysis (Ferenz, 2005).

Since the mid-2000s, Yongyan Li has published a series of articles (previously cited) focusing on the writing and publication attempts of scientists in mainland China. Mostly single case studies, these papers range from computer science (Li, 2006a) to physics (Li, 2006b), to chemistry (Li, 2007a), to biomedicine (Li, 2007b), to management (Li, 2014a), and to medicine (Li, 2014b). Using triangulated data sources and drawing on various theories, such as legitimate peripheral participation, community of practice, enculturation, and socio-political theory, they provide insights into the pressures that Chinese academics are under to publish internationally and the strategies that they use to achieve their goals. A very interesting aspect of Li's case studies is that, as well as revealing the challenges faced by her participants, she is able to reveal the strategies to which they ascribe their successes. For example, in one study of a doctoral student of science, Li (2005) describes how, after an initial rejection from his first target journal, he managed to publish a paper in his second choice. The strategies he described include building up a bank of useful rhetorical and linguistic forms as he was reading the literature in his field. In another study, of another doctoral science student (Li, 2006b), the participant sought help from his supervisor, used the feedback from the journal editor and reviewers, made use of an editing service, and was extremely persistent (to such an extent that he appealed a rejection, before, after six rounds of review, he ultimately achieved success). In her study of a third doctoral science student (Li, 2007a), the participant drew on his previous experience of getting published, which included the importance of organisation and structure, emphasising the positive aspects of the study being reported, getting the right "angle" on the research (p. 66), and using Chinese in organising his thinking. He also cited a paper previously published by his research group (in order to establish his credentials), and borrowed words and phrases from articles he read. This last strategy was studied by Li, this time working with Flowerdew, across a whole group of Chinese doctoral research students (Flowerdew & Li, 2007). They labelled this strategy *language re-use* (see also Buckingham, 2014 on this strategy). As well as providing useful research findings, case studies such as those of Li can provide useful data that can be fed into ERPP training.

Another book-length study using a naturalistic approach (alongside survey research) is Mu's (2020) *Understanding Chinese multilingual scholars' experiences of writing and publishing in English: A social-cognitive perspective*. The book includes four ethnographic case study chapters, each one investigating how an individual Chinese scientist goes about writing for international publication in English. All of the four cases have achieved publication in higher-ranking international journals. The methods used are similar to those already described: text history and talk around text (Lillis & Curry, 2010). Interestingly, Mu includes experienced scholars in his research, as well as novices, who are often the focus of naturalistic ERPP case studies. One of these, a chemist, for example, had already published 165 international papers. Mu employs a socio-cognitive framework based on intercultural rhetoric, cognitive process theory, and constructivism. Based on the case studies and this framework he develops a taxonomy of successful writing strategies, thereby exhibiting the applied nature of much ERPP research.

Other notable studies using the naturalistic approach include those by Casanave (1998), Englander (2009), Mur Dueñas (2012), and Luo and Hyland (2021). What all of these case studies highlight is the complex, situated nature of writing for publication – how it varies according to the context of production – and the complex negotiations, including those of (multilingual) identity, involved in achieving success. The participants and practices involved in these case studies all have their individual characteristics based on geography, culture, discipline, institution, identity, power, individual agency, and other factors and this is one reason why more studies are needed. On the other hand, examples from these case studies can be used in ERPP pedagogy. For example, participants might be asked to consider the three approaches to writing an RA described by St. John – writing first in the L1 and then translating to English, writing first in the L1 and then having the article translated by someone else into English, or writing directly in English – and discussing the merits of each, based on their experience. Or they might be asked to compare the experience of the participant in Flowerdew's (2000) case study with their own. Or they might be asked to consider the various strategies used by the participants in Li's various case studies and discuss their respective merits.

Before leaving this section, we should also mention other qualitative ERPP studies which use interviews, but which do not involve the complex ethnographic methods of the studies we have reviewed (e.g., Canagarajah, 2018; Flowerdew, 1999b; Langum & Kirk Sullivan, 2017; McDowell & Liardét, 2019; Pérez-Llantada, Plo, & Ferguson, 2011). Such studies are useful in providing more targeted data, but they do not provide such a rich picture as do the naturalistic case studies.

Conclusion

In this chapter, we have reviewed two important approaches to research in ERPP: genre analysis and naturalistic studies, starting off by pointing out that the approaches link up with theories presented in the previous chapter – genre theory and social constructivist theory – and that we will be considering more empirical work that has been conducted within the framework of these two theories here. In the sections on genre analysis, we have highlighted Swales's seminal work on the RA genre and reviewed other work in this tradition, including corpus-based approaches. We have also drawn attention to genre analysis that contrasts different discourse styles across cultures. Our assessment of genre analytic approaches is that they are able to reveal the intricacies of form–function relations in academic text as they are created within academic discourse communities and that such descriptions can provide input to a pragmatically oriented approach to ERPP pedagogy. Our review of naturalistic approaches began with an explanation of the theoretical tenets of the approach. We explained that these approaches are more context-oriented and view academic writing as a social practice that is embedded in socio-cultural and ideological structures. Following our discussion of the theoretical tenets, we reviewed a number of studies that have investigated different aspects of ERPP using naturalistic methods. These example studies demonstrate how such approaches can provide a broader understanding of text production and demonstrate how writing for scholarly publication is much more than an issue of autonomous linguistic competence. The results of such studies can feed into ERPP pedagogy in providing exemplars that can be used as case studies in ERPP courses as well as having implications for institutional policies, such as highlighting the need for ERPP training. More generally for the practitioner, the findings of both genre analysis and naturalistic approaches have the potential to contribute to the necessary understanding of the discursive and non-discursive practices of their target learners.

7

GATEKEEPING AND PEER REVIEW

Introduction

The historical development of the concept of peer review was briefly outlined in Chapter 3. In this chapter, we will consider the present-day multifaceted complexities involved in this practice within the broader framework of academic gatekeeping. We will look at the research within ERPP that has examined the practices of those involved in peer review and the discourses of the review process. There is no doubt that gatekeeping is a mysterious process and an occluded practice for many scholars, especially novices. Editors and reviewers lead a double life both as active, visible members of their academic discourse communities and as mysterious ghost figures who can determine the fate of both individual submissions and ultimately the academic careers of their authors. There has been a major growing stream of scholarship within the field of ERPP which has looked at gatekeeping practices and processes. This line of research has tried to demystify the backstage of the publication procedure and shed light on this important dimension of knowledge surveillance. It has brought to the fore the discourses and interactions between authors and gatekeepers, the complexities involved in those relationships, as well as unspoken expectations and perspectives of editors and reviewers. In this chapter, we will first review the purposes and benefits of peer review and then consider editor and reviewer perspectives on the review process. After that, we will examine the question of editor and reviewer bias, which has become a controversial topic in ERPP. In the final section, we will look at genre analysis conducted on editor and review reports.

Purposes and benefits of peer review

The goal of peer review in the context of ERPP is to help decide on the potential of a research article (RA) for publication. It is a self-regulation system operated by

DOI: 10.4324/9780429317798-7

academic journals providing scrutiny by the disciplinary discourse community. It maintains quality and provides credibility. If an RA is published in a journal with a high impact factor then readers can be confident in the reliability of what they are reading. Hyland (2015) adds that it is a democratic and objective procedure. As we said in Chapter 3, moreover, peer review is the basis for other evaluative measures, such as impact factor to measure journal quality and h-factor to measure individual scholarly esteem. An important function of peer review is providing useful feedback to authors. In one survey (Ware & Mabe, 2012), over 90% of respondents believed their most recent paper to have been improved by peer review. In the same survey, in a strong endorsement of the procedure, 84% of respondents thought that without peer review there would be no control in scientific communication. Peer review may also provide guidance to authors on alternative possible venues for their submission if it is not accepted by the original target (reviewers are often requested by editors to recommend alternative journals if they are not recommending publication). From the editor's perspective, peer review provides essential input to the decision-making process. As Leki (2003), herself an experienced editor, points out, it is referees, not editors, who decide on the fate of submissions (although, of course, it is the editor who makes the final decision).

Reviewing is an important responsibility. Reviewers, as anonymous "custodians of knowledge" (Starfield & Paltridge, 2019), not only play a decisive role in determining the fate of an article, but also can ultimately affect individual scholars' academic life courses, in terms of visibility, career progression, and allocation of scholarly funding. It is thus reassuring that in the survey by Ware and Mabe (2012) referred to above, 90% of respondents stated that they reviewed articles because they like playing their role in the academic community and 85% because they like reading new articles and being able to help improve them. This certainly shows a high level of commitment to one's peers and the overall research publication enterprise.

Gatekeepers' perspectives

Given the pivotal role of editors and reviewers, research has tried to throw some light on these arbiters of the academic world. Some studies in this area have looked at the views of editors and reviewers regarding effective writing and publishing. This scholarship can play an important role in demystifying the role of journal gatekeepers. Consequently, it can facilitate the socialisation of novice scholars into the practices of their academic discourse communities and the gatekeeping process. It can also help develop useful pedagogical interventions and support mechanisms for newcomers to scholarly publication. In one such study, Kapp, Albertyn, and Frick (2011) presented the results of a closed- and open-ended questionnaire survey seeking information on reviewing processes, editorial practices, and common errors made by authors. The findings, based on returns from 73 editors, highlighted that style and language, lack of focus, poor contextualisation, non-compliance with journal submission guidelines, research design, and inappropriate content for the journal were the most common challenges and errors among junior scholars. Echoing findings of Ware and Mabe (2012), the 90 editors of international nursing journals in Freda and Kearney's (2005) survey highlighted review deadlines and the poor writing quality of submissions as challenges confronted by their reviewers. In a study using in-depth interviews conducted in Canada, Habibie (2015) sought the opinions of three faculty advisors, three journal editors in education and applied linguistics, and five senior Anglophone doctoral researchers on the issues that novice scholars face in writing for publication. The doctoral student participants argued that novice scholars face various discursive and non-discursive challenges in scholarly publication including:

- unfamiliarity with the journal article genre;
- the rhetorical configuration of its constituent sections;
- lexico-grammatical struggles;
- targeting appropriate journals and negotiating with gatekeepers;
- handling the affective and emotional burden of the review process.

The editors in Habibie's study argued that although the development of scholarly publication literacy requires structured mentorship and pedagogy, those support mechanisms may not necessarily be available for junior scholars in their academic contexts. This can create serious challenges for them if they want to participate in the discourses of their target academic communities.

Focusing on some of the challenges that novice scholars encounter in scholarly publication, Paltridge (2019a), a very experienced editor and reviewer himself, presents a number of strategies that can help junior researchers to understand reviewers' reports, respond to reviewers' comments, and ultimately navigate the gatekeeping process successfully. He argues that novice scholars should bear in mind that reviewer feedback is usually presented in a polite way and may seem like suggestions to junior scholars. However, it is imperative to know that these suggestions should be interpreted as directives for revision and that reviewers expect authors to act on them. Paltridge recommends that junior scholars should not get discouraged by critical feedback and should address peer-review comments systematically and politely. In responding to reviews, authors should deal with all comments, avoid direct disagreement, and explain and justify the changes they have or have not made clearly and politely.

Critique of peer review

Whatever the merits of reviewers and review reports, peer review cannot be claimed as a perfect gold-standard, when reviewers may disagree over a paper and an editor has to decide which of the two are right or has to solicit a third review to create a majority opinion. There may also be bias; reviews are supposed to be blind. They may be single- or double-blinded. In single-blind peer review, the authors do not know who the reviewers are, but the reviewers see the names of the authors. This opens up the possibility of bias. In double-blind peer review, reviewer and author identities are concealed from each other. But even here, in many cases, it is easy for a reviewer to work out who has written a paper, especially in a narrow field where participants are known to each other. So, there is still the possibility of bias. Peer review is fallible in other ways, too. Increasingly, there are cases of retractions of articles from journals, either because of scientific error or even fraud (Steen, 2011; Vuong, 2020). Furthermore, there are many examples of ground-breaking work which was rejected when first presented, while many papers which achieve publication are arguably second rate (Michaels, 2006). Furthermore, the peer-review system is time-consuming and stretches out the publishing process. Modern technology and the globalisation of scholarship mitigate this problem, because editors and reviewers can communicate instantly via email across the globe, but time is still needed to conduct the review and reviewing is not the top priority of scholars.

A final criticism of peer review, and this applies to the whole publishing process, is that academics provide their services without any financial reward. Publishing houses are making considerable profits, but not rewarding those who create those profits. In a world of marketised universities, the workforce is not compensated. It is not surprising, therefore, that editors often have difficulty in finding reviewers. In the era before publish or perish, scholars may have given their time willingly in the pursuit of knowledge and through collegial solidarity. Some may argue that this process, with the pressure of more and more manuscripts to review, is no longer fit for purpose, but no alternative has been provided to date (Hyland, 2015).

Editor and reviewer bias

We have mentioned bias as an issue with peer review; here we will survey some of the ERPP research that has focused on the important topic of editorial bias in the gatekeeping process. One of the issues that makes the review process challenging is that in spite of its textual orientation (i.e., focus on the submitted manuscript), it is a complicated interaction between a group of human beings. In other words, it is an enterprise which involves two groups of people (i.e., gatekeepers and authors) who are intellectually, emotionally, and professionally engaged, each with their own ontological, epistemological, and methodological perspectives. Every single scholar can tell different stories about the peer-review process, their own trajectory, and especially the problems and challenges involved.

What makes bias difficult to detect and remove is that it is often disguised as common sense, so it is invisible. The review process cannot be totally immune to bias and lack of impartiality (Hyland, 2020) and that is why research has also investigated the existence and practice of it. Tomkins, Zhang, and Heavlin's (2017) study of both "single-blind" and "double-blind" models of the review process provides evidence for reviewer bias. The findings indicate that factors such as authors' reputation and their institutional ranking are significantly important for an acceptance decision by single-blind reviewers compared to their double-blind peers. Ross, Hill, Egilman, and Krumholz (2008) also provide evidence of bias in open conference abstract selection, authors from the US, English-speaking countries outside the US, and prestigious academic institutions being favoured at the expense of others. Moreover, when blinded review was conducted for the same conference in subsequent years, reviewer bias was partially reduced.

Accusations of bias against EAL scholars

A main criticism levelled at the gatekeepers of academic journals comes from EAL scholars. Such academics, who labour under "the triple disadvantage of having to read, do research and write in another language" (Van Dijk, 1994, p. 276), may feel that their EAL status and proficiency level in English puts them at a disadvantage and in a vulnerable spot in the review process and subjects them to editorial and peer review "linguistic bias" (see e.g., Belcher, 2007; Canagarajah, 2002; Corcoran, 2019; Martín, Rey-Rocha, Burgess, & Moreno, 2014; Pérez-Llantada, 2014; Ross, Hill, Egilman, & Krumholz, 2008; Strauss, 2019). In Chapter 4, we reviewed various surveys demonstrating how many EAL writers feel themselves to be at a disadvantage in writing for publication in English because, unlike Anglophone scholars, they have to write in an additional language. We can describe this as a case of structural bias (Vanman, Paul, Ito, & Miller, 1997). In parallel to his quantitative survey (reported on in Chapter 4, Flowerdew, 1999a), Flowerdew (1999b) conducted an in-depth interview study with 26 mostly junior Hong Kong Cantonese-speaking scholars, where they elaborated on the specific nature of this structural bias, which they felt put them at a disadvantage vis-à-vis their Anglophone counterparts. They are: less facility of expression; longer time taken to write; a less rich vocabulary; difficulty making claims with the appropriate amount of force; composing process possibly influenced by L1; qualitative articles more problematic than quantitative articles (see also Cho, 2004); and being restricted to a simple style. Such observations may be fostered by the fact that, as reported in many accounts in the literature, reviewers and editors often ask that authors have their paper proofread by a "native speaker" of English (e.g., Clavero, 2010; Pérez-Llantada, Plo, & Ferguson, 2011). Indeed, as indicated in Chapter 4, this is a recommendation of many journals in their submission guidelines. To the extent that this recommendation, even though it may be well-intended, is made only to "non-native speakers" and not to Anglophones, it is certainly an example of structural bias against the former group. The requirement to write in Standard British or American English or "good" English (and not ELF or a variety of World Englishes), as reported also in Chapter 4, is similarly an example of structural bias against EAL writers (Englander & López-Bonilla, 2011; McKinley & Rose, 2018).

In addition to these structural biases, some EAL writers have expressed a belief that they are subject to what has been referred to in the psychological literature as confirmation bias, the tendency to evaluate information in terms of one's existing beliefs (Nickerson, 1998; Oswald & Grosjean, 2004). In this case, these EAL writers anticipate that gatekeepers will evaluate their submissions on the basis of a belief that EAL writers are less capable of writing a publishable article than their Anglophone peers. In Flowerdew's (2000) single case study of a novice EAL scholar in communication studies in Hong Kong, the participant, Oliver (a pseudonym), expressed his concern about such confirmatory editorial bias when he stated that "the journal editor's first impression of your manuscript they discover that it is not written by a native-speaker—no matter how brilliant your idea they will have the tendency to reject" (pp. 15–16). In a more recent study, Corcoran (2019) investigated the contrasting perspectives on English as a language of science and fairness in the adjudication of EAL scholars' research writing. The study involved 55 Latin American scientists and seven North American Anglophone scientific journal editors in health/life sciences. In focus group discussions, the novice and experienced EAL scholars exhibited "pervasive, vigorous claims of inequity" (p. 556), including bias based on author name, institutional affiliation, and/or English-language use. Interestingly, the report on these focus groups included a very similar exchange to the comment made by Oliver in Flowerdew's (2000) study reported above:

Anna: Just reject. And they don't review, they don't check the paper in the same way as it would be [when] written from an English person.
Juana: I have heard the same thing too. I don't know if I's a myth but when they look at a last name and that it's not European or English they say this report is not from an English speaker or something like that and they don't judge the same.
Maria: Yeah.

p. 549

Whether such comments are based on a myth or not, as speculated by Maria in the above exchange, it is disturbing that such beliefs are held by novice researchers in locations as far apart as Hong Kong and Mexico.

The examples of structural biases presented above in terms of specific requirements for EAL scholars to have their work checked by a "native speaker" and to write in an Anglophone variety of English, together with the belief on the part of some novice researchers from Hong Kong and Mexico that they are subject to confirmatory bias in terms of reviewers being prejudiced against them as EAL writers, go some way to explain the use of the term "stigma" to refer to the predicament of EAL scholars by Flowerdew (2008) and Horn (2017) vis-à-vis their Anglophone peers.

It is important to note that the survey data we have reported refer to attitudes, not facts (although some of these attitudes may be based in personal experience). It is certainly the case, however, that editors and reviewers do comment on language. In Belcher's (2007) analysis of 29 reviews of papers sent to the *English for Specific Purposes Journal* over a three-year period, she found that language was the most frequently commented on feature of the texts under review and the feature most frequently negatively commented upon. In their study of peer review of articles in education and psychology in four "periphery" European countries, Lillis and Curry (2015) found that, out of 95 text histories (see Chapter 6 for definition) collected, in 58 (68%) of them, at least one of the evaluators (the editor and/or one or more of the reviewers) "foreground English or language as a significant problem with the article" (p. 134). On this basis, Lillis and Curry concluded that "[f]indings from the quantitative analysis therefore indicate that English and language are indeed construed as a problematic issue" (p. 134). This does not tell us, however, if these comments affected judgements and decisions on publication. In Martín, Rey-Rocha, Burgess, and Moreno's (2014) survey of 1,717 Spanish medical researchers, while the respondents saw the features of their writing in English as the main obstacle to publishing in journals published in English, the main reasons put forward by editors and reviewers for rejection were related to content, not language. Of course, editors of scientific journals are likely to emphasise science over language in making decisions, even if they perceive language to be a problem; they are scientists, not linguists, after all. Another point to bear in mind in discussion of possible bias in peer review is that the published research does not seem to take into account those (many) articles which never reach the review stage (so-called "desk-rejections"). We have no way of knowing what linguistic bias may or may not be exercised in those cases (Corcoran, 2019; Flowerdew, 2019).

The counter-argument against bias

From a different perspective, however, there is another position on bias against EAL writers, which argues that concrete evidence should be presented before such claims can be made (Ferguson, Pérez-Llantada, & Plo, 2011) or which even denies the possibility of identifying systematic bias in the review process (e.g., Hyland, 2020; Lee, Sugimoto, Freeman, & Cronin, 2013). Thus, Hyland (2015) maintains that "[p]eer review is a human process and subject to human imperfections. Bias may exist, but it is often a bias of beliefs and preferred interpretation, rather than bias against certain theories or individuals" (p. 168).

This counter-argument against bias further claims that, in spite of EAL writers' misgivings, the author's first language or proficiency in English is not a decisive factor in the acceptance of a submission and that the quality of language rarely determines the fate of a submission (Belcher, 2007; Bocanegra-Valle, 2015; Coniam, 2012). As Hyland states again, there exists "little evidence to support the idea that there is widespread and systematic bias against writers whose first language is not English" (Hyland, 2016, p. 20). This counter-argument further argues that negotiating the originality and centrality of one's research, or what Swales (1990, p. 7) calls "establishing a niche" or carving a research space and embedding one's research within the broader scholarship, the quality of argumentation, and contribution to disciplinary scholarship are among the key factors that gatekeepers take into account (Gosden, 2003). In other words, the difference is more "between those who know the academic ropes in their chosen specialisms and those who are learning them" (Swales, 2004, p. 56).

Small-scale studies of corpora of referees' reviews by Belcher (2007) and Coniam (2012) lend empirical support to the case against bias, showing that authors' linguistic background and language proficiency are inconsequential to the reviewers' recommendations, which focus more on the content and quality of the research. Furthermore, Paltridge (2019b) argues that "the acceptance of non-standard forms of English in published research articles seems to be increasing, with English-language proficiency no longer being the absolute barrier to academic publishing that it may once have been" (p. 238), a point we discussed in Chapter 4. A caveat which we might add here, though, is that much of the applied linguistics research into peer review has been conducted with data drawn from applied linguistics journals and conducted by editors or regular reviewers from that field (Belcher, 2007; Coniam, 2012; Flowerdew, 2001; Habibie, 2015). Such gatekeepers, as experts in language, are far more likely to guard against linguistic injustice and bias than are reviewers from other disciplines. Furthermore, as Corcoran (2019) comments, "those in positions of power are unlikely to self-incriminate" (p. 552).

Finally, countering the accusations of scholars from Hong and Mexico reported above with regard to bias, there are contrary reports in the literature of EAL writers not experiencing any sense of bias or discrimination. For example, a participant in Shchemeleva's (2021) interview study with 18 social science scholars at an elite Russian university stated as follows: "There's no discrimination. These are the rules of the game we are all playing" (p. 15) and Shchemeleva's overall interpretation of the results of her study was that "[t]he majority of the participants do not seem to feel any unfairness, any bias, or discrimination that was witnessed in some studies of multilingual scholars' research writing practices (p. 15) (see also Cheung, 2010; Cho, 2004).

EAL versus periphery

A complicating issue with regard to the debate regarding linguistic bias is the fact that it is mixed up with (semi)peripheral status (cf. World Systems Theory, Chapter 5). Many, if not most, EAL writers are located in periphery or semi-periphery countries and they may feel discriminated against on the basis of geography as well as language background. In an early report by Gibbs (1995), "Lost science in the third world", many of the more than 100 scientists interviewed referred to "structural obstacles and subtle prejudices" that hindered the transfer and dissemination of scholarship from economically undeveloped to developed countries. Half of the participants thought that reviewers and editors were biased towards them and were "convinced that the gatekeepers of mainstream scientific journals are more likely to reject a paper from an institution in an underdeveloped [sic] country than an article of equivalent quality from an industrial nation" (p. 97). Gibbs (1995) reported that "[a]lthough developing countries encompass 24.1 percent of the world's scientists and 5.3 percent of its research spending, most leading journals publish far smaller proportions of articles by authors from these regions" (p. 93). On the same theme of prejudice against peripheral scholarship, in addition to feeling linguistic prejudice, Flowerdew's (2000) participant, Oliver, felt scholars like him from Hong Kong were discriminated against because of where they come from, on the periphery and outside the academic centre.

> There is the language problem, but there is more than that. Hong Kong scholars submitting to the [United] States are suffering from a lack of common dialogue from the mainstream. What I mean, when I was in the US, although I am a NNS, I don't feel the problem. I speak every day with them certain topics, but when I leave the States I lose that ability to link the hot topic, voice the politically correct voice … It is a circular spiral process … yes, being connected to the leading edge, and the further you get away the more you're not sure what's going on anymore.
>
> *p. 135*

Oliver had studied in a leading research university in the US and, now that he had returned to Hong Kong, he was experiencing Geertz's (1983) "Exile from Eden" syndrome, where young academics complete their studies in leading research universities and then have to leave to go and work in more minor institutions which offer only limited opportunities for research. In this respect, it is worth noting that Geertz had a different periphery in mind to that of Oliver, the US, which has its own centre–periphery, one which Anglophone Americans may experience in their own country just as do EAL international scholars such as Oliver in the international (semi)periphery.

Certainly, it is more difficult to achieve publication if operating outside the centre. Hyland (2016) reports on various studies which demonstrate a lower publication success rate for articles from low-income countries. Patel and Kim (2007) and Saposnik, Ovbiagele, Raptis, Fisher, and Johnston (2014), for example, identify much higher rejection rates for articles from such locations, while Rohra (2011) reports that the percentage of articles from less-developed countries decreases as the impact factor of the journal increases. This does not indicate intentional bias. It may be that conditions for research are more conducive in more advanced countries and more highly ranked universities. A structural bias, built into the system, though, may be that editors prefer more universal topics and are less interested in publishing research focused on peripheral locations. A Hong Kong applied linguistics researcher is reported by Hyland (2016, p. 64), as follows:

> You have to set the study in a bigger context, one that is going to echo with the wider discipline. Nobody is really that interested in what is going on in HK schools, nobody outside HK that is, and you have to put it into their terms. Critical perspectives or how it contrasts to overseas studies.

Furthermore, as Bennett (2014) has reported, research from the periphery may be taken up and reported in the centre (also Ryazanova, McNamara, & Aguinis, 2017), which is perhaps unfair on those periphery scholars who have done the research, notwithstanding that it may contribute to global science.

Remediating the situation

Whatever the truth might be with regard to bias, there is also no doubt that "[w]hile peer-review reports can sometimes be seen as frustrating obstacles to publishing, for junior scholars in particular, the process can be instructive and a valuable form of mentoring" (Hyland, 2015, p. 164). This requires some adaptations and adjustments by both authors and gatekeepers. By the same token, the literature presents a number of strategies and guidelines that gatekeepers can adopt in order to alleviate the challenging nature of this sometimes-unsurmountable academic endeavour. König and Bajwa (2020) underline the importance of "openness among reviewers toward less-than-perfect English writing, particularly by non-native speakers" (p. 54). In spite of the existence of different instructions and guidelines that are meant to inform EAL scholars in negotiating with gatekeepers (e.g., Happell, 2011; Liu, 2014; Paltridge, 2015), König and Bajwa (2020) argue that "following such guidance requires English-language skills that many non-native English researchers may lack" (p. 55). They highlight the importance of a "tolerant" reviewer's clear and precise feedback in enhancing the quality of the manuscript, especially when it comes to raising the author's awareness of problematic linguistic issues. Similarly, Clavero (2010) highlights the significance of raising gatekeepers' awareness of linguistic injustice/bias in natural science disciplines:

> NES scientists, and particularly those involved at any level in the peer-review processes, should become aware of the linguistic injustice problem. They would then probably be more tolerant with the English language inaccuracies of NNES; a simple change in attitude that could alone give rise to a fairer scenario in scientific publications.
>
> *p. 552*

Corcoran (2019) argues in the same vein, as do Köhler et al. (2020) more broadly, highlighting the necessity for "openness toward different research techniques, methodologies, epistemologies, or theoretical foundations" (p. 17). In sum, peer review is a grey area within scholarly publication. However, as Hyland (2015) argues, it seems that currently it is the most feasible gatekeeping mechanism and quality control yardstick if such guidelines and suggestions are integrated into the process.

Genre analysis of peer review

Recent years have witnessed a growing interest in the genre analysis of journal peer-review reports (see Belcher, 2007; Flowerdew & Dudley-Evans, 2002; Fortanet, 2008; Gosden, 2003; Hewings, 2004; Hyland, 2015; Kourilova, 1996; Paltridge, 2015, 2017; Samraj, 2016). Given that this occluded genre (Paltridge, 2017) is off-limits to the public in general and is only accessible to the author and the review team (editor and reviewers) involved in the process, most of the studies in this research strand have been conducted by either existing or former editors of academic journals who, thanks to the affordances of the digitalisation of the review process, have access to the databases and archives of their journals or personal archives of reviewers. In what follows, we will look at some of the findings of this research strand, focusing on some of the discursive characteristics of the review process genre. This line of research concerns the textual analysis of the reviewer's report, examining the schematic structure and lexico-grammatical features of reviews across different disciplines and categories of review report (e.g., accept, revise and resubmit, and reject). In so doing, it sheds light on pragmatic characteristics such as criticism, politeness, and engagement (Belcher, 2007; Fortanet, 2008; Gosden, 2003; Paltridge, 2017, 2020a).

The findings of research in this domain indicate that the peer review report varies in terms of length across different disciplines (Fortanet, 2008) and revise and resubmit decisions tend to be longer than reject or accept decisions (Coniam, 2012; Hewings, 2004). Additionally, the default structure of peer review consists of a summary followed by comments/criticism (Fortanet, 2008; Gosden, 2003), in which criticism is the main and dominant component of peer-review comments (Fortanet, 2008).

Echoing the emphasis on appraisal and evaluation in today's academy that we noted in Chapter 3 and elsewhere in this volume, Paltridge's (2017) book-length study, *The discourse of peer review*, highlights the pivotal role of peer review in a number of occluded genres such as research grant applications, promotion and tenure track applications, and academic book proposals. His main focus, however, is on a corpus of reviews contributed to the journal *English for Specific Purposes*, of which he was for many years the editor. Paltridge shows how evaluative language is essential to reviews, and he exemplifies the use of a range of attitude markers, boosters, hedges, and other stance markers. Many of these markers are used to both create solidarity with the reader through praise, on the one hand, and maintain distance and indirectly remove the writer from responsibility for criticism, on the other. The metaphor of sugaring the pill springs to mind. This was not the case in Kourilova's (1996) analysis of 80 review reports in the field of medicine, however, where there were a great many more unhedged than hedged criticisms. One might hypothesise that the difference in tone between the two studies was due to the fact that Kourilova's reviewers were non-linguists and thus less sensitive to language than those of Paltridge, i.e., there was a disciplinary difference. Alternatively, one might surmise that the difference could have been due to the fact that Kourilova's reviewers were all EAL writers while those of Paltridge were both EAL writers and Anglophones, suggesting that EAL writers are more direct. This second hypothesis is in fact supported when one considers that when Paltridge split his corpus into two sub-corpora of EAL writers and Anglophones, the EALs were found to be more critical than the Anglophones. Clearly, many more studies would be needed to tease out these variables of discipline and language background before being able to come to any clear-cut conclusions. That is not to say, however, that trying to separate them out is not instructive and useful in highlighting the issues at stake.

In spite of the indirect nature of the reviews in his corpus, Paltridge (2017) notes that experienced authors and editors are unlikely to misread the subtle signals typical of reviews. This is far from the case for novice scholars, however, many of whom are likely to have been misled by misleading signals (Kwan, 2013). Mixed signals are a theme of Flowerdew and Dudley-Evans's (2002) examination of the schematic structure and linguistic and politeness strategies of a corpus of editorial letters written by Dudley-Evans as editor of *English for Specific Purposes.* The findings indicated a lack of clarity in the schematic structure of some of the letters and the fact that the editor's criticisms and revision recommendations were framed in an indirect manner, which Dudley-Evans attributed to a desire to save face and show deference to authors. He agreed, however, that this could cause problems of interpretation for readers.

Earlier in this chapter, we mentioned the preponderance of comments on English or language in peer-review reports collected by Lillis and Curry (2015). Frequent comments on language are also to be found in other studies. Mungra and Webber (2010) examined the editors' and reviewers' comments on English-medium medical articles written by Italian researchers and found that, while comments and criticisms regarding the scientific and methodological content of submissions were the most frequent, 44% of comments focused on linguistic errors (lexical and grammatical) and presentation issues (clarity and conciseness). Comments on English in referee reports directed at EAL writers are also frequent in studies by Benfield and Howard (2000) and Mur Dueñas (2012).

This brief review of the literature on peer-review reports shows how genre analysis can inform our understanding of this important gatekeeping genre. In addition to being useful to novice scholars in helping them to decipher reviews of their work, research findings such as those reviewed in this section may be useful in reviewer and editor training, not least if they are able to encourage clearer, but respectful, writing (Paltridge, 2017).

Conclusion

In this chapter, we looked at gatekeeping as a quality control mechanism in the production and communication of knowledge. We began by considering the purposes and benefits of peer review and then considered editor and reviewer perspectives on the review process. After that, we examined the question of editor and reviewer bias. Possible bias is a controversial topic, with some EAL writers believing that they are subject to confirmation bias on the basis that editors and reviewers are prejudiced against them because they are not Anglophones. On the other hand, others, including some EAL writers themselves and editors and reviewers, believe there to be no systematic bias against EAL writers. From another perspective, some feel that there is a structural bias against researchers from the periphery countries. Certainly, in quantitative terms, data shows that it is more difficult to achieve publication if operating outside the centre, one possible factor being that research topics studied in periphery countries may be considered to be parochial. The case has been made for certain measures that might be taken to remediate perceived bias, including more open reviewing procedures and more sympathetic attitudes towards non-standard English. Finally, we looked at a strand of research within ERPP that has conducted genre analysis on reviews and editors' letters, considering the implications of such scholarship for ERPP pedagogy. Gatekeepers are an important cog in the peer-review machine and their efforts and dedication ensures that knowledge and scholarship are evaluated as best as possible. As an under-researched area within ERPP, further research into gatekeepers' (editors and reviewers) experiences, practices, and perspectives is needed.

8

ERPP AND THE DIGITAL AGE

Introduction

In today's world, print is giving way to digital publication and associated technologies. This development is revolutionising the ways in which knowledge and scholarship are produced, adjudicated, stored, and distributed, and is reconfiguring the concepts of audience and authorship (Storch, 2013; Ware, Kern, & Warschauer, 2016; Warschauer & Grimes, 2007). Given the significance and expansion of digital technologies, scholars worldwide need to develop the required literacies in order to have an active presence in cyberspace. They need to equip themselves with the necessary technological knowledge to be able to network and connect within various digital arenas; access reliable sources of data; harvest and analyse relevant information; and record, report, and disseminate the resulting findings in a digital format. They need to do this by means of "communicative genres that diverge from analogue-normative textual conventions" (Thorne & Reinhardt, 2008, p. 561). In this chapter, therefore, we will survey some of the ways in which today's digitalisation is creating a different global scholarly environment and culture. More specifically, we will be looking at how scholarship is constructed and communicated in new ways; how academic communities connect and share content differently; how identities are co-constructed and projected differently; and how the digitalisation of scholarship is presenting new affordances and challenges.

To do this, we will adapt Appadurai's (1996) global cultural economy model and apply it to the digital academy. Appadurai's model consists of five "flows", or "scapes", to account for how people, technologies, capital, information and images, and ideas and ideologies are carried around the globe. These flows, or scapes, are referred to respectively as ethnoscapes, technoscapes, financescapes, mediascapes, and ideoscapes. In this chapter, we will adapt these flows to the international scholarly

DOI: 10.4324/9780429317798-8

publication context and posit four flows, as follows: ethnoscape, epistemoscape, genrescape, and pedagoscape. Accordingly:

- Ethnoscape (Greek *ethnos* 'nation' + Greek *skapos* 'view') concerns how digitalisation has made the concepts of community and membership at the same time more salient and more dynamic, stretching them beyond traditional spatio-temporal boundaries.
- Epistemoscape (Greek *epistēmē* 'knowledge' + Greek *skapos* 'view') deals with the role of digitalisation in transforming the concepts of information and knowledge, the implications of these transformations for literacy, learning, and the construction and communication of knowledge, as well as the risks and challenges that digitalisation has given rise to.
- Genrescape (French *genre*, 'kind, sort' + Greek *skapos* 'view') addresses the influence of digital technologies in the emergence of multimodal genres and practices in different stages of scholarly publication.
- Pedagoscape (Greek *paidos* 'boy, child' plus *agogos* 'leader' + *skapos* 'view') concerns the pedagogical aspect of scholarly publication and how digital technologies have been used to reveal and demystify its inner workings.

Ethnoscape

Digitalisation has had a huge impact on the ethnoscape of the culture of scholarly publication, changing and reconfiguring the concept of academic discourse communities as well as the ways in which the members of such communities exist, socialise, network, and interact. Online presence and social visibility are one of the requirements of the digital age. The nature of academic communities in the 21st century is very different from what went before. Academic communities now stretch beyond spatio-temporal boundaries. Unlike past communities, that were to a large extent confined within certain geographical, temporal, or institutional borders and limited to immediate members within specific territories, the affordances of modern digital technologies have blurred those constraints, deterritorialising academic tribes (Becher, 1989) and extensively extending our imagined scholarly communities (Anderson, 2006). The internet, the most ubiquitous and normalised of the new technologies, has played a pivotal role in bridging the gap between so-called (semi)peripheral and core academic communities, creating a contact zone (Pratt, 1991) that is available for cultural and academic exchange, offering voice and greater visibility to under-represented and marginalised scholars and writers, assuming that they have the necessary digital resources, which is not, of course, a given.

In addition to generic social media platforms such as Facebook, Twitter, and Instagram, and dozens of social media apps such as WhatsApp, Skype, Zoom, Telegram etc. that mediate the social existence, presence, and visibility of all-comers, social media dedicated to scholarly and academic communities such as Google Scholar, LinkedIn, Researchgate, Figshare, academia.edu, and mendeley.com have created online and virtual communities and spaces where millions of academics can connect and stay in touch with other members of their academic discourse communities. These platforms provide international scholars in every corner of the world with the chance to network with like-minded people, enabling them to:

- gain international recognition;
- distribute news and information about new developments in their field;
- share their scholarly and academic achievements, projects, and publications;
- post questions;
- receive publication and citation alerts and notifications on how many times their publications have been read or cited;
- freely share their publications with those (semi)peripheral scholars that may not have or have limited access to the content they are interested in.

In this way, scholarly publication has become transnational and intercontinental, where, thanks to the affordances of various textual and audio-visual (a)synchronous technological innovations, scholars who may have never or rarely met each other in person have the opportunity to engage in collaborative writing, editing, feedback, and research. A good example is this very book, which is the result of collaborative work between two scholars from different continents, Europe and North America. Such collaboration is much easier between the advanced Western countries, it should be borne in mind. Third World countries may suffer from poor internet access, without which international collaboration is not possible. In addition, because the great majority of journals included in the *Web of Science* (see Chapter 3) and other international databases are located in the advanced English-speaking countries, journals from low or middle-income countries (especially those written in local and national languages) receive little exposure and consequently few citations. In a vicious circle, because of their low citation rates, these journals are unlikely to ever be included in the international databases, thereby marginalising the participation of low or middle-income countries (Salager-Meyer, 2014). As Gibbs (1995) predicted, therefore, the internet may have a negative impact and "perversely widen and exacerbate the information gap between the poorest countries and the rest of the world" (p. 94).

Epistemoscape

Digitalisation has played a significant role in redefining the global information economy and this is equally true in the epistemoscape of scholarly publication, that is to say, the ways in which academic knowledge is accessed, distributed, and managed. One of the benefits of the digital age (at least in the advanced democratic countries) is the unrestricted flow of information. Thanks to the affordances of the worldwide web and high-speed internet, problems of access to state-of-the-art scholarship are not a primary concern for many researchers (at least in well-resourced academic institutions).

There is no doubt that the 21st century is the era of information. A comparison between the ways in which knowledge was created in the past and the present brings to the fore the fact that in the past, as Siemens (2005, p. 1) has put it, "information development was slow" and "[t]he life of knowledge was measured in decades" (p. 1). Today, on the other hand, Siemens (2005) continues, "[k]nowledge is growing exponentially [and] [i]n many fields the life of knowledge is now measured in months and years" (p. 1). In other words, "the time span from when knowledge is gained to when it becomes obsolete" (Gonzalez, 2004) has become very short. In this dynamic situation and with this explosive amount of information, a key question becomes "[h]ow can we continue to stay current in a rapidly evolving information ecology?" (Siemens, 2005, p. 4). There is no easy answer to this question. However, it is clear that this "rapidly diminishing knowledge life in our time" (Gonzalez, 2004) requires a different view and model of knowledge development and literacy.

Siemens (2005) highlights the interconnected and networked nature of knowledge production and communication in current times. Pointing out that "[c]haos is a new reality for knowledge workers" (p. 4), he presents a connectivist paradigm of the modern knowledge system and its production and dissemination processes and explains the cyclical nature of knowledge flow:

> Personal knowledge is comprised of a network, which feeds into organizations and institutions, which in turn feed back into the network, and then continue to provide learning to individuals. This cycle of knowledge development (personal to network to organization) allows learners to remain current in their field through the connections they have formed.
>
> *p. 6*

Thus, connections and networks are vital in the construction and communication of knowledge. Networks include information nodes that can be both other individuals/communities or sources of information. The more one has access to these nodes, or what Siemens (2005) calls "small worlds of knowledge" (p. 6), the more knowledge one can develop. In fact, an important dimension of literacy in such a knowledge system is the capability to develop those connections and networks, which can become even more crucial than knowledge itself. In Siemens's words, "[t]he pipe is more important than the content within the pipe" (p. 7). In the same vein, another dimension of literacy is locating those knowledge nodes. That is why "[k]now-how and know-what is being supplemented with know-where (the understanding of where to find knowledge needed)" (p. 2). Finally, in addition, the ability "to draw distinctions between important and unimportant information is vital" (p. 5).

With this in mind, it is clear that digital technologies play a pivotal role in the current knowledge landscape and in scholarly publication as an integral component of the knowledge economy. They both form and provide access to knowledge nodes and facilitate the flow of information in knowledge pipelines. They also reshape and reconfigure our learning and literacy behaviours in order to deal with the epistemic requirements of our time. As Siemens (2005) explains, again, "[t]echnology is altering (rewiring) our brains" (p. 1), and digital technologies that we are using are constituting and shaping our mental processes. All of this, of course, emphasises the need for good internet access not only in the advanced countries, but also the middle- and low-income countries referred to by Gibbs (1995) and Salager-Meyer (2014) above.

More specifically, with regard to the role of technology in transforming the epistemoscape of scholarly publication, that is to say, access, distribution, and management of knowledge, technological innovations have been of great service in storing, classifying, and disaggregating information and knowledge that can be used in academic writing and publishing. Anyone with access to a computer and Wi-Fi can dig into Open Access or subscribed databases such as Google Scholar, Scopus, Eric, and ProQuest (to mention a few). With only limited knowledge and expertise in digital technology, scholars can locate huge mines of resources, sift through them, harvest what they want, and satisfy their quest for relevant information. Discipline-specific databases have made scholarship more accessible and the affordances and digital functions of these databases allow scholars to not only download and save information, but also share it with other members of their academic discourse communities via a mouse click. Digital technologies have also facilitated immediate and easy access to e-book repositories where soft copies of many books can be ordered, downloaded, or borrowed. Similarly, digitalisation of library resources and services and interlibrary loan agreements and protocols such as RACER (rapid access to collections by electronic requesting) have put almost every resource at the fingertips of those interested in them and have played a significant role in proliferation and access to Open Access and subscribed academic journals at any time of the day or night, wherever one might be.

Digitalisation has provided invaluable information and data that can help navigate the publication process. Browsing the public domains and websites of academic journals, scholars have the opportunity to access a range of information, including the aims and scope of their target journals, impact factors, appropriate guidelines and instructions regarding policies, stylistic preferences, submission requirements, review processes, ethical considerations, copyright, and the editorial board of the journal. They can also identify the most downloaded articles, see calls for special issues, or download open-access RAs. Additionally, SCImago Journal & Country Rank portal[1] and Ulrichs Web[2] are two of the important bibliographic directories and databases that can help scholars to attain various sorts of information regarding academic journals and periodicals, such as the year a journal began publication, number of issues/volumes per year, impact factor, national or international rankings, as well as whether the journal is suspected of being a predatory journal. Such detailed information gives academics a nuanced picture of the journal(s) in their disciplines and helps them in targeting the appropriate venues for their publications. International publishers such as Oxford University Press, Elsevier, Springer, and Wiley have also set up alert and feed systems that interested readers can subscribe to and stay abreast of current scholarship and hot-off-the-press or even pre-press output.

Technological initiatives, especially the internet, have also transformed the ways in which scholarly publications are distributed. Since its advent in 1990, the Open Access (OA) movement has provided a new and alternative financial model to established commercial publishing, which has led to the emergence of a different kind of publisher, such as *Public Library of Science* (PLoS) and *PubMed Central* (PMC), thereby facilitating unpaid and democratic availability and access to scholarship for a wider readership. In this model of publishing, journal articles are freely accessible to interested users in two different formats: Gold and Green OA. In the Gold model, all publications are freely available and there are no subscription fees. Journals gain their income by charging universities or individuals. In the Green model, there is also Open Access, but authors deposit their manuscripts, either published or not, in a repository. In this mode, authors can share their papers on their personal websites or university repositories.

In spite of all its benefits, the use of technology in scholarly publication is not without its risks and concerns, and a major risk is related to the pay-to-publish models, especially the Gold OA model. The unquestioning publish or perish ideology of the current neoliberal academy and its strict regimes of audit and evaluation, on the one hand, and the availability in some institutions of monetary resources for research and publication, on the other, have spurred the mushrooming of dubious and predatory publishers and journals, as referred to in Chapter 2. The term "predatory" (Beall, 2010) was originally introduced to refer to deceptive Open Access journals which solicit and publish articles for a fee, with little or no peer review. However, the concept "predatory" has more recently been extended to refer to dubious and scam activities in other knowledge-sharing practices including conferences, book publishing, and more broadly, poor-quality publishing (publishers who fail to offer editorial services, charge fees, etc.). By minimising or removing the peer-review phase (see Chapters 2 and 7) from the overall process of publication, these journals/publishers either trap those uninformed academics who desperately need scholarly publications in order to enhance their CVs or attract unethical opportunist academics who are looking for fast, easy publications. In either case, the result can be poor-quality and often plagiarised output. Jeffery Beall, the founder of Beall's searchable directory of predatory publishers,[3] which is now discontinued and archived because some of the publishers on his list threatened defamation lawsuits against him, highlights the consequences of predatory publication for honest members of the academic community. Honest scientists stand to lose the most in this unethical quagmire. When a researcher's work is published alongside articles that are plagiarised, that report on conclusions gained from unsound methodologies, or that contain altered photographic figures, it becomes tainted by association. Unethical scientists gaming the system may be earning tenure and promotion at the expense of the honest ones (Beall, 2012).

In spite of the problems and issues related to OA publication (see Björk & Solomon, 2012; Davis & Walters, 2011), this model of publication can increase the impact of research, through expediting the publication process and facilitating knowledge mobilisation among all members of academic communities, especially those off-networked scholars in peripheral academic contexts. OA can also play an important role in the review process. As Hyland (2020) argues, it seems that the affordances of OA and new technologies such as distributed ledger technologies (DLTs) can not only centralise the review process and help overhaul "a dysfunctional system", but also support the post-publication review process (PPRP) model as a means of capturing a wider scholarly measure of research quality and impact. In this alternative model:

> papers are published immediately after a light check by an editor, then appointed referees and anyone else contribute reviews which are published next to the article with the name and affiliation of the reviewer. Authors can then either write rebuttals or try to address problems and reviewers can also address these problems,
>
> *Hyland, 2020, p. 60*

Data management is also one of the areas within the epsitemoscape that has been influenced by digitalisation. Nowadays, the affordances of cloud technologies such as Google Docs, Dropbox, Google Drive, and OneDrive facilitate the uploading of a huge amount of information online without the burden of storing it on a computer or a hard disk. This in turn facilitates access to information from different access points (computers, laptops, tablets, smartphones), not merely individuals' computers. Once uploaded, documents can be shared with others and access rights can be set, thereby determining what can be done with the shared information. Open source and paid citation management technologies such as EndNote, Mendeley, RefWorks, Zotero, and Papers (to mention just a few) also provide researchers with the freedom to store, categorise, and retrieve relevant textual, audio, and video files, annotate the literature in various forms, link resources stored within those technologies, as well as search and import related resources from external databases. They also give scholars the opportunity to integrate citations into their texts as they write and to put together a complete reference list based on their chosen format (e.g., APA, MLA, Chicago, etc.) at a few mouse clicks, thereby reducing the bother of manually formatting in-text and reference list citations. Data management has also been key for the publicity and success of academic journals and their publishers on the competitive international market. As "[p]ublication success is not now counted in terms of numbers of subscribers but numbers of downloads of an article" (Paltridge, 2020b, p. 3), publishers and journals are now using the affordances of digitalisation to keep track of the number of hits/views/reads/downloads that an abstract, an article, or a book chapter has received, an indirect strategy in promoting academic products.

Data analysis has similarly become digital. Digital statistical technologies such as SPSS, Stata, and R have long been widely used in different social sciences and natural sciences disciplines and have helped researchers in quantitative data analysis. Similarly, other software and applications such as Nvivo and MaxQDA have been used by scholars in different stages of qualitative and mixed method inquiry, providing researchers with the opportunity to engage individually or collaboratively in data transcription, coding, analysis, and visual presentation. Additionally, Open Access corpus and genre analysis tools such as AntConc and AntCorGen allow scholars, especially EAL scholars, to create personalised disciplinary corpora and analyse and explore discursive nuances within and across their corpora for the benefit of their writing (see Chapter 6). Alternatively, they can use the academic component of large general corpora, such as British National Corpus (BNC) and Corpus of Contemporary American English (COCA), both of which are available online with web interfaces and which contain discipline and genre-specific sub-corpora.

Genrescape

Traditional text has also evolved and been enhanced by means of technological advances. Digital technologies have revolutionised the genres through which we create, submit, and adjudicate content. The emergence and popularity of digital genres such as blogs and wikis has helped promote interaction between authors and audiences (Vandergriff, 2016) and provided scholars with a unique opportunity to disseminate their work to a broader general readership. Although the integrity and credibility of such practices are open to debate and considered "unacademic" and "untrustworthy" by many academics, they have opened a public forum and provided a venue for a socially broader discourse.

Hyper-textuality and multimodality are also two of the important affordances of digital technology in modern times, where publications are not merely mediated through text but can include other media, modes, and genres (Pérez-Llantada, 2016; Sancho Guinda, 2015). Although many academic journals are still more conservative in this respect, many academics and some journals such as *Kairos: A Journal of Rhetoric, Technology and Pedagogy* and the *Journal of Visualized Experiments* (JoVE) have welcomed the "visual turn" (Purdy, 2014), combining visual and aural modes (see Hafner, 2018) and various semiotic resources (images, pictures, etc.). This makes meanings and creates scholarly works that integrate "a plurality of signs in different modes into a particular configuration to form a coherent arrangement" (Kress, 2010, p. 162).

In the traditional sense of writing, technologies such as spell- and grammar-checkers, online-as-you-write dictionary look-ups, and citation management applications integrated into word processing software have become normalised and even taken-for-granted as part and parcel of academic writing and word processing nowadays. These innovations provide accessible and on-demand knowledge and information about spelling formats, word meanings, and synonyms, especially for novice and junior scholars who are new to the discourses and practices of their disciplines. Simple normalised technologies such as track changes have turned feedback, editing, and correcting into taken-for-granted side tasks of academic writing for many scholars. The dictation function of Microsoft Word and

Pages (Mac word-processing software) is a huge help for scholars who are disabled or even prefer to dictate rather than type. The audio-comment function of these programmes has also added another dimension to the medium in which people can leave or exchange audio reminders and comments on their texts. Similarly, the integration and compatibility of these programmes with citation management programmes such as Mendeley, Zotero, and Papers allow scholars to cite on-the-go, as well.

Finally, digitalisation has transformed the submission and review procedures for almost all international journals, in that both processes have become fully computerised and online, employing universally defined stages and moves. Everything from manuscript submission to the review process, negotiation with gatekeepers, right through to the final publication can be done and traced through online portals such as the ScholarOne Manuscript Submission System. This has created a uniform and streamlined picture of the publication process and centralised the constituent stages of scholarly publication for both authors and gatekeepers.

Pedagoscape

The affordances of digital technologies have given publishers the opportunity to add an instructional dimension to their policies and practices and implement online resources and interactive support mechanisms and initiatives. This has helped extensively in demystifying the inner workings and the know-how of the publication process, especially for novice and junior scholars, which required a lot of effort, time, and experience to decipher in the past. These services can not only help more experienced contributors in their scholarly publication practices, but also instruct less experienced, junior scholars in a wide range of areas related to scholarly writing and publishing. They can mentor them in different aspects of academic productivity and scaffold the acquisition of the necessary academic literacy skills set, in order to socialise them into the practices of their target discourse communities. For example, Springer offers a "Journal author academy" module on its public domain[4] which features interactive online courses on two overarching areas: writing your manuscript and submitting and peer review. This module also offers complementary information on Open Access and how to review an article. It furthermore includes "Springer English Academy", which focuses on topics such as: *Why publish in English?*; *Why is good writing important?*; *Reader expectations*; and *Overcoming language barriers*. Each course consists of a number of modules that focus on either writing or publishing components of academic publication, and offers useful, detailed information on various aspects of academic writing and publishing.

Similarly, Elsevier, a very large publishing house, provides an "Early Career Researchers" module on its website, which features training resources for scholarly writing and publishing. It presents webinars, posters, and information on live scholarly publication workshops that Elsevier has presented/will present in different countries. They focus on a wide range of topics, such as academic writing, structural organisation of the journal article genre, targeting appropriate journals, the peer-review process, ethical aspects of research, and Open Access. These resources provide novice researchers with useful information on academic writing and the complexities and intricacies of the publication process. An important dimension of the pedagoscape is corpus-based teaching and learning, which is becoming increasingly popular in ERPP (Chen & Flowerdew, 2018). We refer readers forward to Chapter 9, *ERPP pedagogy*, for more on this application.

Some caveats

In case this chapter has been too positive in tone, we should emphasise some of the downsides of digital technologies and the internet. These mostly come down to the fact that not all scholarly communities are benefitting to the same extent from the digital affordances we have been describing. We have already pointed out above the fact that many journals are excluded from the international indexes and hence are less accessible and we have also highlighted the problem of predatory journals (although this is not actually a problem of access). Obviously, only well-resourced libraries can afford to subscribe to all of the e-journals and e-books that a scholar might need, which is another important caveat. In 2020, the first author of this book contacted Suresh Canagarajah and asked him to what extent the non-discursive issues which were excluding Sri Lankan scholars in the 1990s, as described in his paper and book (Canagarajah, 1996, 2002), still applied today. He replied (personal communication, 1 April 2020) that I was right in surmising that he was in touch with his Sri Lankan colleagues by email (he is now based in the US) and that he had learned that more resources are now available for them. However, there are still problems. Those he mentioned related to the internet are as follows:

- There is electronic access to journal articles, but not e-books.
- Available journal articles are only those that are voluntarily posted by some authors.
- Some publishers are preventing scholars from posting their publications.
- Because of these situations, the knowledge of local scholars is "spotty". They don't have a full understanding of a particular specialisation or method in order to write a publishable article.
- Despite the (limited) online resources available, physical interaction with international scholars is still necessary for networking and developing an insider knowledge of the field. As a result, Sri Lankan scholars do not know how to make sense of the (limited) publications that they are able to download.

No doubt, similar problems are prevalent in other off-network contexts.

Conclusion

In this chapter, we have highlighted how digitalisation has transformed the current landscape of scholarly publication. The pace of change is sometimes so fast that it makes it hard to keep abreast of it, but scholars are adapting to the new requirements of the modern digital order and developing different scholarly habits. We have looked at this transformation in terms of four streams or flows: ethnoscape, epistemoscape, genrescape, and pedagoscape, accordingly, we have seen how digital-isation has created and provided access to virtual academic communities that exist beyond one's immediate spatio-temporal constraints (ethnoscape). We have explored how the nature and very concept of knowledge has been transformed in the era of the worldwide web (epistemoscape). We have looked at the ways in which digital-isation has made scholarly publication a multimodal practice and how "the integra-tion of digital tools has brought the use of different semiotic resources, modalities, and media to the forefront of today's communication practices" (Elola & Oskoz, 2017, p. 54) (genrescape). And we have discussed the affordances of digitalisation for the pedagogy of scholarly publication and the ways in which novice scholars can develop the required literacies by drawing on those affordances (pedagoscape). At the same time, throughout, we have emphasised that many of the benefits of digit-alisation are spread unequally and middle- and low-income countries/off-network scholars are missing out. In this regard, in the final section, we have highlighted some caveats which need to be applied to the advantages of using the digital tech-nologies we have described and the fact that many academics have no or limited access to the affordances offered by digitalisation.

Notes

1 www.scimagojr.com/index.php
2 www.ulrichsweb.com/ulrichsweb/faqs.asp
3 https://beallslist.net
4 www.springer.com/gp/authors-editors/journal-author/journal-author-academy/15186

9
ERPP PEDAGOGY

Introduction

Pedagogical support of various forms can be invaluable in helping novice (and more experienced) academics achieve success in publication. Perhaps surprisingly, however, most scholars receive no formal pedagogical input to the publication process (Kapp, Albertyn, & Frick, 2011; Murray, Thow, Moore, & Murphy, 2008). It is usually a case of sink or swim and learning through experience (Keen, 2007). That is not to say that there has been a dearth of pedagogical initiatives which can be drawn on. Nearly two decades ago, within the domains of health, education, and related disciplines alone, McGrail, Rickard, and Jones (2006) identified 17 studies published between 1984 and 2004 which examined the effects of interventions aimed at increasing publication rates of academic staff. A more recent survey by Li and Flowerdew (2020) focusing on ERPP interventions led by language instructors, and hence aimed primarily at EAL writers, reviewed 31 published studies reporting on such initiatives published between 2004 and 2019. Furthermore, recent edited collections have focused on new initiatives to promote pedagogical responses to increase writing productivity and higher rates of publication (Aitchison & Guerin, 2014; Carter & Laurs, 2017; Corcoran, Englander, & Muresan, 2019). In this chapter, we will use Kwan's (2010) model of the discursive task as a point of departure to identify some of the necessary constituent competencies of that model for successful communication of one's research. We will then show how the model can serve to provide a useful framework in designing ERPP tasks. Following that, we will outline the various modes of delivery for ERPP pedagogy (supervisor mentoring; self-help manuals; course books; courses and workshops; writing groups; and writing retreats), before describing the main methodological approaches (task- and genre-based pedagogy; corpus-based approaches; and critical-pragmatic approaches). In a final

DOI: 10.4324/9780429317798-9

short section, we will say something about ERPP teacher education, a neglected area to date.

Defining the pedagogical task

In an earlier review article on ERPP, Flowerdew (2013a) posed the question:"What should go into a course designed to prepare novice writers, especially EAL writers, in writing for publication?". He answered this question by referring to a model of ERPP competencies by Kwan (2010). Kwan divided these competencies into two main phases:"communicating one's research through an RA" and "communicating with gate-keepers about the RA". Although these phases are distinct, they are at the same time interlinked, because both of them require the ability to write. The two terms correspond approximately to the terms *discursive* and *non-discursive* used elsewhere in this book, although not exactly. In communicating one's research through the research article (RA), the first phase, a number of individual competencies are required, according to Kwan (2010). They include familiarity with the prototypical schematic structure of the genre and its parts (which are subject to disciplinary variation and variation across journals); command of discipline-specific citation language "to advance various rhetorical goals" (p. 57); and metadiscourse "that signals one's degree of commitment to statements made" (p. 57). These particular skills are in addition to general writing skills such as "argumentation, coherence-building and abstracting" (p. 58).

Regarding the second phase, "communication with gate-keepers", Kwan emphasises that this involves what Swales (1997) refers to as "occluded" genres (as mentioned in previous chapters, occluded genres are those not visible in the public domain), which can be "difficult to handle" (Kwan, 2010, p. 58). Reviewer comments tend to be indirect and can be misleading to the reader, as we saw in Chapter 7 (Flowerdew & Dudley-Evans, 2002; Gosden, 2003; Paltridge, 2013). There is thus a need to develop the ability to interpret these documents, on the one hand, and to develop "discursive tactics to carry out revisions accordingly" (Kwan, 2010, p. 58), on the other. Although Kwan does not mention it, there is also a need to know how to write a cover letter to go with an article submission and how to write a response to the reviewers when resubmitting a revised article (which will almost inevitably be needed). Again, these are occluded genres.

In addition to the two dimensions discussed thus far, Kwan's competencies framework for writing for publication has two further elements, both of which merit attention. The first of these is "strategic research conception". Here, the writer needs to ensure that, first, the research is conceived and conducted with appropriate disciplinary theoretical and methodological rigour, and that, second, it finds a niche in the literature in conformity with the "zeitgeist" (Berkenkotter & Huckin, 1995) of the field, fitting into what elsewhere Bazerman (1980, pp. 657–658) refers to as "the conversations of the discipline". Moreover, according to Kwan, researchers need to consider the relevance of their research to the international community. This can be particularly difficult for off-network scholars. Indeed, off-network scholars in

HSS fields, in particular, who may focus their research on local matters, need to consider how they can make their publications appeal to an international readership (Flowerdew, 2001) (see Chapter 7 again). It might also be added here that peripheral researchers need to be able to decide what is appropriate for international publication and what is more appropriate for a local readership (Flowerdew & Li, 2009; Li & Flowerdew, 2009; Lillis & Curry, 2010) (see Chapter 4). Furthermore, publishability will depend on the "fit" between a given article and the targeted journal.

The second additional competence identified by Kwan she refers to as "strategic management of research and publishing". Here, novice researchers need to consider how to manage their research and publication in such a way as to fit in with assessment schedules and the type and number of publications expected by their institution at various academic ranks. To do this, these young researchers need to appreciate the length of time required to produce a manuscript and for it to go through the review process. They also need to know which journals to submit their work to and which journals to redirect their work to in the case of rejection. Indeed, it might be added that they need to know that rejection is the norm for most submissions and that initial rejection does not preclude resubmission, a common misapprehension on the part of novices. Novice scholars also need to know how to deal with rejection from the emotional point of view. Flowerdew (2013a) created a diagram to represent Kwan's model, as shown in Figure 9.1 (adapted). There are other dimensions that might be added to Kwan's model, such as working with academic brokers such as authors' editors (Lillis & Curry, 2010) and collaborating with colleagues or co-authors on a joint paper, but the framework might serve as a useful aide-memoire in the ERPP curriculum design task.

Communicating one's research through an RA
  - command of schematic structure
  - command of discipline-specific citation language and metadiscourse
  - command of generic writing skills (e.g., argumentation, coherence)

Communicating with gatekeepers about the RA
  - command of occluded genres

Strategic research conception
  - command of disciplinary theoretical and methodological rigour
  - ability to find a "niche"
  - ability to relate appropriately to the international community

Strategic management of research and publishing
  - manage time cycle
  - ensure required amount of publications
  - know appropriate journals

FIGURE 9.1 Schematic representations of Kwan's model of the discursive task

Source: Based on Kwan (2010)

The discursive task

Modes of teaching and learning

As Aitchison and Guerin (2014) have stated, "[c]learly, there can be no one simple approach to developing and supporting scholarly writing. The act of producing text and of writing is a complex, situated, social and political act that makes and reflects identity, position and power" (p. 38). We will thus review a variety of modes of teaching and learning in this section, including mentoring by PhD supervisors; self-help manuals and course books; courses and workshops; and writing groups and retreats.

Supervisor mentoring

In the traditional model of doctoral education, the student is mentored by a supervisor (advisor in the US), who is responsible for their study (Catterall, Ross, Aitchison, & Burgin, 2011; Parker, 2009). There is a general understanding in the international academic community that academics are taught to write under the tutelage of their supervisors (Maher & Say, 2016; Paré, 2011). In a survey conducted in a large science, health, and technology faculty among 29 supervisors and 36 students, Catterall et al. (2011) found that "feedback on student writing was universally regarded as the primary pedagogical tool for teaching and learning research writing and for most, the supervisor's role was central to this" (p. 2, abstract).

Indeed, one way that novices can learn to write is by co-authoring with their supervisor (and/or their peers). Co-authoring is, in fact, the preferred model in the laboratory-based disciplines. As Thomson and Kamler (2013, p. 160) state, "[w]riting together is hands-on learning about writing for publication per se. It's not talking about writing for publication as an idea—it's the reality". Furthermore, collaborative writing divides the workload and helps the development of inexperienced writers through working with more experienced authors (Keen, 2007). Collaborative writing with a supervisor, as does the overall supervisory model, fits in very well with apprenticeship theories of situated learning and legitimate peripheral participation (see Chapter 4) (Beaufort, 2000; Hasrati, 2005). As a caveat, however, where students write with supervisors, there are ethical and power issues at stake to do with relative contributions and ordering of names in the published article (Keen, 2007) (see Chapter 3 on this topic).

In spite of the benefits of the supervisory model, as Aitchison and Guerin (2014, p. 31) write, "Increased workloads of supervisors, the growth of interdisciplinary, multi-method research and cross-institutional studies mean that the previously tight fit between student and supervisor is increasingly less likely". Furthermore, many academics do not feel they have the necessary skills to provide writing support for their research students (Aitchison & Guerin, 2014; Catterall et al., 2011; Paré, 2011). This is especially the case as regards EAL students, where supervisors may well not understand the particular difficulties of their multilingual students. The idea of publishing prior to graduation is also new in many cases and supervisors have not been prepared or trained for facilitating this requirement. Although efforts are being made to improve the supervisory model (Aitchison & Guerin; 2014; Keen, 2007; Kiley, 2009; Lee & Kamler, 2008), because of its deficiencies in helping students with writing for publication, many students have had to rely on trial and error, peer assistance, learning through reading, or self-help manuals (Catterall et al., 2011). As a result, attention has turned to finding solutions outside the supervisory model for preparing students to write for publication (Catterall et al., 2011). As Aitchison and Guerin (2014) write, "[a]s the primacy of the supervisor-student dyad is disrupted, suites of other opportunities are being made available to doctoral students, including workshops, seminars, disciplinary and institutional conferences, masterclasses, coursework programs and so on" (p. 32). We might add that, because many academics have often not been prepared for writing for publication during their own doctoral study, there is also a demand for these other solutions among even experienced scholars.

Self-help manuals

Given the lack of formal training in ERPP, many aspiring scholars have recourse to the plethora of available self-help manuals (e.g., Belcher, 2009; Curry & Lillis, 2013; Day & Gastel, 2006; Driscoll & Driscoll, 2002; Glasman-Deal, 2010; Heard, 2016; Kamler & Thomson, 2006; Keen, 2007; Moore, 2003; Murray, 2013; Paltridge & Starfield, 2016). These books vary in content, but usually provide guidance on how to write clearly, concisely, and persuasively, how to structure the various parts of the RA, and how to go about the submission and peer review process. They may also include advice on planning the research, conducting the literature review, drafting and redrafting the article, and research and publication ethics. Specific advice on language varies, depending on whether the book is primarily targeted at EAL or Anglophone writers. If the former, it may include a focus on academic vocabulary, grammar, cohesion, and coherence. These manuals are sometimes also used as course books or supplementary reading for courses. The guide by Curry and Lillis (2013) is interesting because it is focused on the larger social practices, politics, networks, and resources involved in academic publishing and how to formulate and situate research and gain access to publication in international refereed journals; there is no focus on language. This guide, however, is aimed at the social sciences, particularly education and psychology.

Course books

There is only a limited number of volumes specifically designed as course books for ERPP teachers to choose from. They can also be used for individual use. They are mostly targeted at EAL writers and have an overt focus on language. The best-known of these is Swales and Feak's (2012) *Academic writing for graduate students*, which is not designed specifically with writing for publication in mind, but the most recent edition has more emphasis on the research article. The volume is very much based on applied linguistics research and takes a consciousness-raising, genre approach, also using insights from corpus linguistics (see below on these approaches). Swales and Feak also published a manual targeting dissertation and research writing, *English in Today's research world: A writing guide* (2000). However, this volume has now been divided up into separate booklets devoted to abstracts, introductions, literature reviews, and supporting genres.

Another, more recent, contribution is Cargill and O'Connor's (2013) *Writing scientific research articles*, which is aimed overtly at writing for publication. Cargill is a well-known ERPP researcher who has run ERPP workshops in many countries and O'Connor is her scientist collaborator who co-teaches some of the workshops with her. The book is developed out of the authors' experience in running these workshops, Cargill's theoretical knowledge of applied linguistics and language teaching, and O'Connor's experience as a published scientist. The book uses the IMRaD structure to organise the chapters, although, interestingly, they are ordered according to how the authors judge a typical scientist would work on an article – i.e., results, method, introduction, discussion, title, and abstract – not as they appear when published. Advice is also given about manuscript submission and communicating with journal editors. Furthermore, guidance is provided on criteria used by reviewers when evaluating manuscripts and on how to deal with reviewers' comments, manuscript revisions, and resubmissions. Finally, the authors show how to use sentence templates and how to use concordancing software in the writing process.

Courses and workshops

In the introduction to this chapter, we referred to the 17 studies published between 1984 and 2004 on ERPP interventions in the field of health and related issues reviewed by McGrail, Rickard, and Jones (2006). Of the 17 studies, the provision of a course was the second most popular format, with seven courses reported on in six studies, after writing support groups, which had eight studies, each reporting on a single writing group initiative. However, courses included both single block workshops lasting 1–2.5 days and extended series of 90–180-minute sessions running for up to eight weeks. The courses were led by experts, who were usually senior academics or professional editors. Participants were provided with didactic and written information about the writing and publication process, usually produced internally. The sessions were run by either internal staff or invited journal editors. Common topics included how to write for a particular audience; how to select appropriate journals; tips for dealing with writer's block; knowledge of the submission and reviewing process; and conceptualising ideas for writing. Flawed examples of writing were discussed, as well as published material. Examples of responses to reviewers' comments were also included in some courses. In courses run over an extended period, participants were able to present parts of a developing manuscript from one session to the next, with the goal of arriving at a complete manuscript at the end of the course. In workshop-type block session courses, some sort of writing was also usually required. Another feature of some courses was sessions run by invited journal editors to discuss what they look for in a publishable paper and reasons for reviewers' recommendations and decisions. All of the courses surveyed included some form of evaluation, including in the form of publication outcomes, and all courses achieved positive outcomes in terms of publication success. As a caveat, it should be borne in mind, however, that a course is unlikely to be reported in an international journal if it has not met with some degree of success. The courses surveyed by McGrail, Rickard, and Jones (2006) were all conducted in Anglophone countries (Australia, Canada, UK, US) and directed at Anglophone participant writers, with no allowances made for EAL writers. They therefore did not focus on linguistic features such as grammar, lexis, cohesion, or coherence, although the ongoing practical writing would presumably have provided opportunities for feedback on such features, as long as the course instructors were able to provide it.

If we turn now to the survey conducted by Li and Flowerdew (2020), the focus of this study was on courses offered by language teachers, so they all targeted EAL participants, although some did also include Anglophones. Li and Flowerdew (2020) describe the methodological approaches employed in the courses reported upon. Genre-based pedagogy (Cheng, 2018; Swales, 1990) was frequently applied. Courses using this methodological approach were typically organised following the IMRaD structure of the empirical RA, that is, teaching units were organised around one of these genre parts. They used a task-based approach, with published RAs employed as learning input and used Swales's (1990) rhetorical consciousness-raising approach. Another feature of some courses, although a minority, was a critical-pragmatic approach (Corcoran, 2019; Corcoran & Englander, 2016; Flowerdew, 2007) (For readers not familiar with the methodological approaches referred to in this paragraph, they will be explained in a later section of this chapter.)

Li and Flowerdew (2020) highlight a number of challenges encountered by ERPP teachers, as reported in the literature they reviewed. One of these was heterogeneous classes involving participants from different disciplines, a way to deal with this potential problem being to turn it into a virtue in allowing participants to compare and contrast how their respective disciplines would deal with a given feature. A related issue was the difficulty in dealing with specialist content in their course participants' disciplines. One solution to this issue is to involve a content specialist in the teaching, a procedure adopted by Cargill and O'Connor, as referred to above. Failing that, instructors can make it clear to participants that, although they do not have the content knowledge that their participants do, they are nevertheless knowledgeable in being able to analyse the discourse of the students' discipline, what Ferguson (1997) refers to as "specialised", as opposed to "specialist", knowledge, the latter term referring to knowledge of the disciplinary content. Making participants aware that the instructor is themself involved in research also provides face validity. Also problematic in many courses was a lack of time to cover the necessary ground required. A solution here was to help participants develop autonomy and gain control of the process of producing an RA through planning, setting achievable targets, self-monitoring, and proactively seeking and engaging with peer feedback, important skills in themselves for a successful academic career.

Li and Flowerdew (2020) also highlight the fact that the language-focused courses they reviewed gave less emphasis to Kwan's (2010) "communicating with gatekeepers" aspect of ERPP. They provide a useful list of features that might be added to the courses they reviewed, as follows:

- publishing ethics (including plagiarism);
- how to select appropriate venues for publication (including discussion of impact factors and predatory journals);
- how to deal with gatekeepers (reviewers and editors);
- how to work with language brokers of various kinds, an important feature of real-world EAL writing for publication (Lillis & Curry, 2010) (including the issue of ethics in working with editing services);
- how to work in writing teams (most journal articles are authored by teams rather than individuals, especially in the science and technology disciplines);
- how to make use of online resources (although this was referred to in some reports);
- how to ensure maximum impact for an article following successful publication.

Writing groups and writing retreats

A writing group is composed of like-minded students or academics who meet together for the purposes of working on or improving their writing and providing mutual encouragement (Cargill & Smernik, 2016). Working within the framework of community of practice (Benvenuti, 2017), writing groups may involve the sharing of ideas, peer critique, and actual writing. A writing retreat is an extension of this concept, but can take place away from the usual study context and may be over an extended period of time (Murray & Newton, 2009). It allows PhD students and early-career researchers who are under pressure to complete their thesis or publish the opportunity to take time out to focus on their writing (Paltridge, 2016).

Writing groups and retreats are becoming increasingly popular, a phenomenon which Guerin and Aitchison (2017) attribute to "the rapid growth and diversification of doctoral research students and programmes globally, in turn requiring new responses from institutions and supervisors" (p. 51). A possible contributing factor, these writers speculate, could be "the simultaneous and independent movement for self-help and community-building by doctoral students, often via online technology" (p. 51).

Guerin and Aitchison (2017) classify writing groups and retreats into critique-focused and productivity-focused writing groups. Critique-focused writing groups can be facilitated by language experts, supervisors, or peers. Participants in these groups discuss their writing, guided by the group leader. Productivity-focused writing groups focus on actual writing. Periods of intense silent writing are interspersed with shorter periods of conversation. They may take place in public spaces, such as cafes, or may be in more extended residential retreats, or *boot camps*, a day or more of intensive writing.

Methodological approaches

Methodological approaches are concerned with what goes on in the classroom. Within the ERPP literature, a number of methodological approaches are prominent: task- and genre-based pedagogy; corpus-based approaches; and critical-pragmatic approaches are the main ones.

Task- and genre-based pedagogy

A task-based approach to pedagogy is one in which participants are asked to perform tasks that resemble real-world activities, as opposed to more traditional language-learning exercises, such as vocabulary memorisation, grammar pattern practice, or dictation (Ellis, 2003; Nunan, 2004). In an ERPP course, this would mean the use of authentic RAs as input, rather than artificially simplified texts; the provision of appropriate linguistic scaffolding so that the participant can complete the assigned task; active learning with maximum participant involvement; participants working together; and an emphasis on form–meaning relationships. A genre-based approach to pedagogy (Hyland, 2007), which goes together with a task-based approach, employs tasks involving the analysis and creation of a genre or genres. The goal is to establish in the mind of the learner systematic links between the communicative purposes (as expressed by moves and steps) and linguistic properties of texts. Cheng (2018) describes the procedure as follows:

> The approach is discovery-based, with learning scaffolded by the instructor by means of open-ended questions regarding the rhetorical context, organizational pattern, and lexicogrammatical features of a given instance of a genre, which may be compared and contrasted with other similar texts (RAs) in a process of rhetorical consciousness raising.
>
> *p. 91*

Rhetorical consciousness raising is an approach which involves drawing attention to form–function relations in the various moves and steps of a genre. The idea goes back to Swales (1990). Such consciousness raising allows students to see the kinds of rhetorical and linguistic devices that typically make a text accessible to them; they are first made aware, or conscious, of the new language, then they recognise and distinguish it, and finally are able to produce it. Swales wrote that "there may be pedagogic value in sensitizing students to rhetorical effects, and to the rhetorical structures that tend to recur in genre-specific texts" (p. 213), adding that, in teaching the RA:

> [w]e can ... recognize that students are helped if they can also schematize the structures of the [IMRD] sections themselves and so further develop an understanding of what it is that allows them to recognize a section as Method or Discussion, and what it is that allows them to argue that one section is more or less effective than another.
>
> *p. 213*

Later, Feak and Swales (2010) formalised this procedure into a cycle of four steps: Analysis, Awareness, Acquisition, and Achievement. As well as allowing for raising consciousness regarding the context and lexico-grammatical features of the moves and steps of a genre and its wider communication purpose, this procedure encourages a critical reflection on the process. Pérez-Llantada (2015) suggests that the procedure can be extended to compare instances of genres in English with similar genres in learners' L1s in order to create further awareness through comparison and contrast. Construing rhetorical consciousness raising as a form of metacognition, Negretti and McGrath (2018) investigated how genre knowledge and metacognition can be scaffolded in a genre-based course for doctoral students engaged in writing RAs. The output on two genre-related tasks and post-task interviews showed how participants used "facets of genre knowledge metacognitively in their writing, by describing how they engage with reader expectations, conventions, variation, and the possibility of strategic deliberate choices" (p. 218, abstract).

Consciousness raising can be employed in various types of learning tasks, such as discussing the results of genre analysis, *metacommunicating* (talking about instances of a genre), participants doing their own genre analysis, translating, and using corpus tools on a corpus of RAs (see below) (Flowerdew, 1993).

Corpus-based approaches

A corpus is a collection of texts held in electronic format that can be searched to identify commonly recurring language patterns. An appropriate corpus is a very powerful tool in the hands of the ERPP teacher. When we say an appropriate corpus, we mean that the corpus should be made up of RAs in the appropriate discipline(s) and of sufficient number to afford reliable linguistic and rhetorical generalisations. A corpus can provide a way into the writing practices of the target discourse community (Burgess & Cargill, 2013). It can be searched by inputting a word or phrase to produce a set of concordances, that is to say, all of the lines of text in which the original search term appears in the middle, surrounded by its immediate context. Teachers can highlight for the learner authentic examples of general academic or more specific disciplinary usage. For example, Burgess and Cargill (2013) show how in an ERPP workshop they demonstrated to their participants the preferred patterns of the word *role* with different prepositions in the field of biotechnology. The following are the findings they shared on the basis of a corpus search conducted along with their participants:

- The three common prepositions are *for, in,* and *of* (*role + for/in/of*).
- The type of noun after the preposition seems to be the key difference:
  - *in* is followed by a noun of process or a verb + -ing (*a role in management/a role in managing ...*)
  - *for* and *of* are followed by a noun representing a chemical or similar, and commonly have a subsequent *in* phrase representing the process (*a role for enzymes in breaking down food particles / the role of enzymes in breaking down food particles*)
- The preceding verbs are also distinctive:
  - *suggest* and *indicate* before *role for* (*suggest a role for / indicate a role for*)
  - common use of *play* before *role in* (*play a role in*)

To take another example, Chen and Flowerdew (2018) showed participants in one of their ERPP workshops how they could find different ways to describe a table in an RA. A corpus search provided a range of different verbs which are typically used, examples being *show, see, give, list, summarise, compare,* and *indicate.* These words were then looked at individually to see what phraseological patterns they appeared in, some examples being as follows:

- *Table X shows;*
- *...is/are shown in Table X;*
- *Table X lists;*
- *...is/are listed in Table X;*
- *Table X summarises;*
- *...is/are summarised in Table X;*
- *Table X indicates;*
- *...is/are indicated in Table X.*

At a more basic level, a frequency list of the vocabulary in a corpus can be created. This is useful as a starting point for further searches to see how chosen words from the list are used in context. Teachers may also use the corpus to confirm or disconfirm their own intuitions about a particular usage pattern. This is important when working in disciplines with which the teacher is not familiar. ERPP courses using corpus tools are usually integrated with a genre-based approach (Chen & Flowerdew, 2018; Cotos, Link, & Huffman, 2017; Dong & Liu, 2020; Eriksson, 2012). The tools can identify the linguistic patterns associated with the various moves and steps of a genre to facilitate rhetorical consciousness raising.

Corpus tools can also be very powerful in the hands of learners themselves and there are examples of ERPP courses which show participants how to use such tools as an aid to writing. In this approach, which is referred to as data-driven learning (DDL) (Johns, 1991), the student, with guidance from the teacher, takes control of the learning and investigates the properties of a corpus of language (research writing of some sort in the case of ERPP) to assist with their own writing. The investigation is conducted by means of corpus queries such as those described above. An important use of the procedure is as a checking device, where the user compares a feature of their own writing with what is to be found in the corpus. If the user's usage is not found in the corpus, so long as the corpus is an appropriate one in terms of size and discipline, then it is likely that it is not appropriate. The user may then try other wordings until they find an appropriate one. Instead of using a published corpus or one created by the teacher, participants may be shown how to create their own corpus, based on RAs from their own field. This ensures that they will be accessing data which is authentic to their specific purposes.

Li and Flowerdew's (2020) survey of ERPP courses explicitly excluded those that focused on corpus-based approaches. In another survey, however, Chen and Flowerdew (2018) reviewed 37 empirical studies from the year 2000 on corpus-based approaches in the academic writing classroom, many of which focused on ERPP courses. Lee and Swales (2006) describe a course where their participants were introduced to this approach, as do Cargill and O'Connor (2006), Charles (2015), and Chen and Flowerdew (2018). It should be noted that there have been some criticisms of DDL in terms of the time and effort it takes learners to become proficient in the use of the tools and findings are mixed regarding their long-term use after training (Charles, 2014).

Critical-pragmatic approaches

While the three methodologies we have described above could also be described as classroom techniques, the critical-pragmatic approach to ERPP pedagogy (Corcoran, 2019; Corcoran & Englander, 2016; Flowerdew, 2007) is both a technique, but also, more importantly, a philosophical approach. It encourages a consideration of the political issues at stake with regard to international publication in English, which we have reviewed in earlier chapters of this book. Drawing on debates in the mainstream EAP literature and a paper by Harwood and Hadley (2004), Flowerdew (2007) contrasted three possible socio-political positions with regard to ERPP pedagogy: pragmatic, critical, and critical pragmatic. Pragmatic approaches prioritise helping participants to comply with the academic conventions in order to do their best in the publish or perish game; critical approaches encourage a questioning of the status quo and inequities in research publication, for example alerting EAL writers to the difficulties and disadvantage of their community due to the hegemony of English and encouraging more publication in local journals and languages; while critical-pragmatic approaches represent a middle way, assisting in the achievement of the necessary goals, but at the same time encouraging the development of a questioning attitude towards what is being demanded. This last of the three options encourages scholars to have "a critical mind set" (Flowerdew, 2007, p. 23) at the same time as making them aware of "possible repercussions of some of the critical actions" (Flowerdew, 2007, p. 23), for example, arguing with an editor over features of non-standard English might lead to rejection of a paper.

The idea of the critical-pragmatic approach has been taken up by Corcoran and Englander (2016), who later relabelled it as critical-plurilingualism (Englander & Corcoran, 2019), to emphasise an approach which values the co-existence of several languages in research publication, not just English. These authors argue that there would be three key components to a critical-pragmatic/critical-plurilingual approach: (1) raising genre awareness (drawing attention to the situatedness and temporality of genres); (2) raising critical language awareness (notions of power, gatekeepers, multiple ways of knowing, language and identity, plurilingualism); and (3) sustainable writing practices (developing advocacy, networks of literacy brokers, disciplinary support, etc.). Corcoran and Englander (2016) suggest that pragmatic features of standard ERPP courses could be modified to take in more critical dimensions which would highlight "the intersections of language, power, and identity in the production of academic knowledge" (p. 261). For example, an introductory session on the scientific RAs as a means of communicating with particular discourse communities could also discuss the politics of language choice within the global market of knowledge production; a focus on rhetorical elements of a scientific RAs could also discuss English as a Lingua Franca and how rhetorical, lexico-grammatical, and stylistic features may be taken up by gatekeepers; a focus on stylistic elements of a scientific RAs could also discuss this in relation to identity and author voice; and a focus on navigating the review process of journals could consider the global politics of publishing with regard to access, scope, etc. (Corcoran & Englander, 2016).

To conclude this section, we present two perspectives based on experience with the critical-pragmatic approach. In her account of her 15 years' experience using a critical-pragmatic ERPP approach with social science students, Cadman (2017) is highly committed to the critical-pragmatic approach, as indicated by the following quotation:

> To me, it has been conclusively demonstrated that this kind of transcultural critical pragmatic ERPP pedagogy works effectively to engage a learner's situated, intellectual and affective position as a researcher … [It] also raises their doubts, frustrations and resistances, and encourages them to articulate these to each other and to me in trusted dialogic exchanges.
>
> *p. 48*

In a reflection on two iterations of a critical-pragmatic ERPP course offered to humanities doctoral students at the University of La Laguna, Tenerife, Spain, Burgess, Martín, and Balasanyan (2019), while emphasising their responsibility to raise students' awareness of linguistic injustice in international research publishing, are more sceptical on its outcomes, stating that:

participants were interested in what we had to say about questions of equity and social justice in relation to languages of research publication and presentation; however, of greater concern to them was their immediate need to learn as much as they could about the accepted or normative conventions of ERPP and to acquire the necessary skills to meet these conventions.

p. 137

As previously mentioned in Chapter 3, a more critical approach may appeal to some teachers and learners more than others, depending on their personal philosophy, politics, and discipline.

ERPP teacher education

Li and Flowerdew (2020) report in the conclusion to their survey of the literature on ERPP courses that their focal literature had little to say about any training, if any, that the ERPP instructors had received; they surmised that any training was most likely informal. This is probably the case, because teacher education for ERPP has yet to develop (although see Li & Cargill [2019] for an interesting innovation in the field). Swales (2019) speculates on the predicament of the typical EAP teacher confronted for the first time with teaching an ERPP course. She (sic) most likely has a Master's degree in applied linguistics or a related field (not a PhD), he muses, will not have published an article herself or reviewed for a journal, but will be expected to assist doctoral students write journal articles and show them how to get them published. If we accept Swales's model of the prospective ERPP teacher (and his model is perhaps unrealistically neophyte), what might such a teacher do? As a first step, she might read this book. But, hopefully, in the not-so-distant future, she will be able to attend a workshop, if not a course, to develop some practical, as well as theoretical, ERPP skills. Teacher education is therefore an important next step for the field of ERPP pedagogy.

Conclusion

In this chapter, we began by pointing out that most scholars receive no formal pedagogical input to writing for publication in English. This is in spite of the fact that such support can be invaluable and that various pedagogical initiatives have proved to be effective. In the main body of the chapter, we first considered the nature of the ERPP pedagogical task, highlighting two important dimensions: communicating one's research through the RA and communicating with gatekeepers. We then reviewed a range of modes of delivery (supervisor mentoring; self-help manuals; course books; courses and workshops; writing groups; and writing retreats). After that, we examined several methodological approaches that are commonly employed in ERPP pedagogy (task- and genre-based pedagogy; corpus-based approaches; and critical-pragmatic approaches).

From the review presented in this chapter, it is clear that the range of knowledge and skills required of the ERPP teacher is demanding. We concluded the chapter, however, by pointing out that ERPP teacher education is sorely lacking and this is likely an important next step for ERPP as a field of research and practice.

10
CONCLUSION

Introduction

ERPP has now established itself as a fast-expanding field of research and practice within English for Academic Purposes (EAP) and the broader discipline of applied linguistics. A key driver behind this volume has been a desire to highlight this development, to delineate the scope of this new field, and present a state-of-the-art review of the relevant literature to date. A similar desire lay behind the creation of the *Journal of English for Research Publication Purposes* (co-edited by Pejman Habibie and Sue Starfield) in 2020, to recognise ERPP as an established field and to create a dedicated forum for reporting research and practice within it. As the chapters of this book have shown, the range of topics and issues that ERPP is engaged in makes it an interdisciplinary field whose boundaries extend beyond EAP and applied linguistics, to embrace disciplines including (in alphabetical order) anthropology, discourse studies, economics, education, history (of science), information technology (IT), linguistics, oriental studies, policy studies, politics, postcolonial studies, psychology, rhetoric, sociology, sociology of science, and writing studies, all of which have left their mark on the developing field. This interdisciplinary nature of ERPP is a positive aspect for researchers and educators, encouraging research in scholarly publication beyond traditional disciplinary boundaries and framing the construction and dissemination of knowledge as a situated socio-political and ideological practice that has both local and global implications.

When the first-named author of this book applied for a research grant to study the scholarly writing practices of Hong Kong Chinese academics in the lead-up to the transfer of sovereignty from the United Kingdom to China in the late 1990s, there was little literature in which to situate the research proposal and a heavy reliance was put on Swales's (1990) *Genre analysis: English in academic and research settings*. Twenty five years or so later, in 2021, as evidenced by the reference list in this

DOI: 10.4324/9780429317798-10

volume, we have a wealth of knowledge – about the political economy of English as the international language of research and publication; about the benefits and the drawbacks for EAL scholars of writing for publication in English; about the discourse of research English; about the publication processes and the roles of editors and reviewers; about the ways scholars go about writing for publication and their interactions with various academic brokers and other stakeholders; about the role of technology in scholarly publication; about how to go about the teaching of ERPP; and many other aspects.

In this concluding chapter, we will first sketch out some of the areas we have not had time or space to deal with in enough detail. We will then review some of the areas and issues that are ripe for further ERPP scholarship. After this, we will consider the place of ERPP in the university of today, both in terms of policy and practice. Finally, we will briefly speculate on the future of ERPP and English as the language of international research and publication.

Limitations of the volume and opportunities for further research

In introducing the field in this volume, we have tried to cover as much of this ground as possible. However, for reasons of space (or ignorance) there is much that we have left out. For example, in our focus on the research article (RA), as the preeminent genre of the academy, we have not had space to deal with other genres which belong to the writing for publication genre set (Swales, 2004), that is, those genres which interact with the RA, leading up to it, following on from it, or existing alongside it (see Chapter 6). These genres, which we have mentioned but not dealt with in great detail, include the PhD thesis/dissertation, the writing of which has an extensive literature of its own (e.g. Paltridge & Starfield, 2020). As we have indicated in previous chapters, publication is increasingly occurring at the same time as thesis/dissertation writing and there are important discursive and non-discursive interactions between the two which can also fall within the scope of ERPP. Another genre we have neglected is the conference presentation, which we only mentioned in passing as a genre interacting with the RA (see Chapter 6 for references). This is arguably in some ways an even more challenging genre than the RA for the novice (especially EAL novice) scholar, because it carries with it the emotional burden of speaking in public that perhaps does not attach to the written genres (see La Madeleine's account, for example, of the nervous Japanese post-doctoral researcher reported in Chapter 4; see also Ramirez-Castaneda, 2020). A whole set of genres we have not dealt with is new media/digital genres (Kuteeva & Mauranen, 2018; Pérez-Llantada, 2016) – how some traditional print genres have become digital, how some genres have evolved into new digital hybrids, and how new genres are emerging (Luzón & Pérez-Llantada, 2019). One of these new genres is the blog. Whether or not blogs are a research genre is an open question, because they are concerned with communicating and recontextualising scientific research findings for diverse audiences of both specialists and non-specialists. Particular writing skills are needed, nevertheless. Bloggers are required to tailor key findings of relevance to the audience in a less formal style than that of the RA (Luzón, 2013). Blogs may certainly be considered as part of the toolkit of writing for publication, if not the main tool, the RA. It is the case that we have given some attention to the occluded genres of the editors' and reviewers' reports and the grant proposal in previous chapters, but we could have said more. As for (co)authored and (co)edited books, book chapters, conference proceedings, and book reviews, we will have to leave it to others to review ERPP research on those genres, which is admittedly relatively scant (but see Hyland, 2009).

With regard to our treatment of the RA, there are also some limitations which we should point out. We have perhaps been too rigid in our description of its structure. It is true that in the natural sciences the IMRaD pattern is very common, although, as we have stated in Chapter 3, some natural science disciplines, including maths, diverge. In humanities and social sciences (HSS), however, there is much more variation, which we have not had time or space to explore (see e.g., Tusting, McCulloch, Bhatt, Hamilton, & Barton, 2019). Furthermore, we have not stressed the variation in personal style that can occur, especially in the HSS disciplines (Tusting, McCulloch, Bhatt, Hamilton, & Barton, 2019), but also in the natural sciences (Hyland, 2012; Negretti & McGrath, 2020). More broadly, we have not considered the variation in beliefs, values, assumptions, and conventions which characterises the different disciplines and consequently their approaches to writing for publication (Becher, 1989; Becher & Trowler, 2001) and the fact that disciplines are in a constant state of flux and internal diversity and conflict, with interdisciplinarity becoming the norm (Trowler, Saunders, & Bamber, 2012). Scholars writing for publication need to go beyond an ability to replicate the established formal patterns of the RA in their discipline, to develop a generic competence (Bhatia, 2004) which is sensitive to the beliefs, values, and assumptions of their discourse community and their target audience and journals, while at the same time not denying their individuality. This topic certainly merits further investigation and certainly needs to be carried over to pedagogy.

There are some academic mediating roles that we might have devoted some space to. We are talking here about authors' editors, translators, and proofreaders. We have reported in Chapter 6 on the naturalistic research which has highlighted the role of academic mediators. Indeed, the notion that writing for publication is a distributed competence and not that of a single author even if only one name appears on a published paper is one of the important findings of ERPP research. However, we have not delved into the individual contributions that these mediators play (see Matarese [2013, 2016] on the role of authors' editors; also, Flowerdew & Wang [2017] for an empirical study; see DiGiacomo [2013] on the role of translators; also, Na & Hyland [2019] for an empirical study; see Harwood, Austin, & Macaulay [2009], and Turner [2011] on proofreading).

Having highlighted some areas where we might have done more in the book, let us turn to areas where there are gaps in the field offering opportunities for further research. Although there is a great amount of genre analysis being conducted on the RAs, there is likely to be a lot more, if only because discourse analysis and corpus especially are very popular subjects and topics for PhD work. In Chapter 5, we have already highlighted some gaps in this literature. As corpus tools become more sophisticated, it is likely that further inroads will be made into establishing form–function relations at the move level and above, as already begun very promisingly by e.g., Cotos and her associates (see Chapter 6 for references). Work is also in its early stages with the new media genres and studies are needed which document how the RA itself is evolving, not least due to multimodal and online innovations. Research is also needed into how the affordances of digital tools are affecting scholarly communication more generally, in terms of facilitating collaboration, on the one hand, and online text creation, on the other (Hafner & Pun, 2020). Furthermore, although the tools of genre analysis have held up well to date in analysing the new media genres, there may be a need to combine the more traditional textual methods of analysis with naturalistic, situated, ethnographically oriented approaches (Flowerdew, 2011), in order to see just how scholars go about using these media (see McGrath [2016] for such a study).

There are opportunities too in intercultural discourse studies. While we know something about the discourse styles, in terms of rhetoric and logical argument, of various cultures (especially European ones) (see Chapter 5 for references), less is known about others. Such research does not need to be limited to the level of text, but may also embrace the whole issue of knowledge construction across cultures. Do Indonesian scholars, for example, tend to go about conducting research and publication in the same way as Americans do? The studies by Li (2005, 2006a, 2006b, 2007a, 2007b, 2014b) of the research practices of Chinese natural science scholars, for example, suggest that they have a different way of going about things as compared to their Western counterparts. This brings us to the need for naturalistic studies of writing for scholarly publication in more diverse settings than those we currently have. There are many studies set in various European countries, in some Asian countries, and in some South American countries. Further studies from these regions are still needed, of course, but we know little if anything about writing for scholarly publication in the majority of African countries, in the countries of the Middle East, and in Russia, although a first (to our knowledge) ERPP study set in Russia has recently been published (Shchemeleva, 2021).

With regard to naturalistic approaches, again, there is scope for alternative directions and methodologies. A number of scholars have already used personal accounts to examine their own scholarly publication trajectory within the broader socio-political context. We have referred a number of times in earlier chapters to the work of Canagarajah (1996, 2002), which is seminal in that regard, where he looked at his (and his colleagues') scholarly publication practices as multilingual scholars in the context of the Jaffna, Sri Lanka and then after his immigration to the US. Casanave and Vandrick's (2003) edited collection is another example that comes to mind, where established scholars in the field of applied linguistics and language education provided autobiographical narratives of their academic and writerly trajectories. Casanave (2019) and Mur-Dueñas (2019) have also used the analytical lens and elements of auto-ethnography/autobiographical narrative to look at their scholarly publication experiences. More work using this approach would be well received and is indeed in progress (Habibie & Burgess, forthcoming; Habibie & Hultgren, forthcoming; Hultgren & Habibie, forthcoming). Adopting auto/duo/trio-ethnographic methodologies, Habibie and Burgess (forthcoming) use a (dialogic) narrative approach to bring to the fore scholarly publication practices of both Anglophone and EAL early-career scholars in different inter-national academic contexts. Similarly, Habibie and Hultgren (forthcoming) use the same narrative approach to look at the practices of gatekeepers of international academic journals in different geo-linguistic contexts. In the same vein, some of the auto-ethnographically oriented chapters in Hultgren and Habibie (forthcoming) focus on women scholars as an under-researched and under-represented popula-tion in ERPP scholarship and examine how hegemonic discourses and practices dominating today's academy as well as global events such as the COVID-19 pan-demic disadvantage female scholars in different international academic contexts and marginalise their participation in the construction and dissemination of knowledge.

It is worth mentioning again that Anglophone scholars and the Inner Circle are still an under-represented and under-researched population and context in ERPP scholarship and research approach (Habibie, 2019). Further naturalistic and ethno-graphically oriented research into scholarly publication practices of both main-stream and off-network Anglophone scholars (especially doctoral students and novice scholars) can provide a multifaceted, complementary, and comparative view of the experiences and challenges of these academics in scholarly publication and consequently enrich the ERPP knowledge base. It can also inform the tailored development of useful pedagogical policies and practices that can benefit this demo-graphic in their participation and contribution to the global knowledge economy.

The above are just some of the directions in which further research in ERPP might go. Of course, it will also be necessary to incorporate the findings of the above suggested future areas of research into practical applications to ERPP peda-gogy and ERPP teacher education.

ERPP in the university

Identity and positioning of ERPP

In spite of the increasing expansion of ERPP scholarship, it seems that more work is needed for greater recognition of the key role that ERPP can play in current academia. Because of the fact that ERPP is an offshoot of EAP and there is a lot of overlap between the discourses and practices of the two fields, the domain, scope, aims, and applications of ERPP scholarship may still not be clear enough for many academics and not be well-perceived in many academic contexts. Given the current neoliberal regime dominating the academy, the pivotal role of scholarly publication in the institutional business model (Blackmore & Kandiko, 2011), and the serious implications of scholarly productivity for scholars globally, academic institutions and universities need to recognise the critical role that ERPP can play to help their faculty members and students to develop the required literacies for scholarly publication. While there is a "growing provision (and demand) for ERPP instruction worldwide" (Li & Flowerdew, 2020, p. 38), it is not clear in which part of the university this provision and demand should be met. Is it in the language centre, in the writing centre, or in the academic department or faculty?

At the policy level, universities need to develop thorough and structured measures and strategies that mandate the instruction and mentorship of writing for scholarly publication. In spite of the extensive pressure for publication, especially for doctoral students and novice scholars, writing for scholarly publication or ERPP instruction is not a core or even side constituent component in the curriculum at undergraduate or postgraduate levels in many disciplines (Burgess et al., 2019; Cameron et al., 2009; Messekher & Miliani, 2019; Murray & Newton, 2008). The literature not only indicates the significance of English-medium scholarly publication as a requirement for graduation or as a prerequisite for the oral examination of the thesis in different academic contexts, but also the lack of or very limited provision of ERPP instruction, usually under the pretext that the required literacies will naturally flourish as a result of the doctoral programme, as highlighted in Chapter 9.

The development of structured mandates and policies for the provision of ERPP education in the university curriculum requires a comprehensive understanding of the needs of those for whom such an education is provided. In other words, it is important that academic institutions see novice scholars and graduate students as "a unique population of students with unique needs" (Philips, 2016, p. 159). In-depth needs analysis may help the development of clear and organised policies and curricula, which in turn can delineate the ways in which ERPP instruction can be provided. For example, they can specify whether ERPP instruction should be part of the curriculum of graduate programmes and be offered as a core/optional ERPP course; as a component of another doctoral course such as research methodology; or in the form of short-term professional development workshops or seminars where invited speakers, usually faculty members, present their experiences and insights regarding academic writing and publishing. They can also specify the ways in which faculty members and supervisors should mentor junior scholars for developing scholarly publication literacies and determine the responsibilities of both faculty instructors and students. Additionally, academic institutions need to specify point departments and people for the provision of ERPP services and tailoring appropriate pedagogies and content for the instruction of ERPP and the provision of ERPP support. There is no doubt that clear, coherent macro-level institutional policies which are informed by ERPP research and scholarship can play a pivotal role in the development of appropriate and structured pedagogical practices and ultimately scaffold the socialisation of newcomers into the academy and the discourses and practices of scholarly publication.

ERRP in practice

Academic institutions also need to have a very focused approach at the peda-gogical level. Such an approach can inform the pedagogical practices of course instructors and supervisors, the services offered by writing/support centres, and type of courses dedicated to ERPP. However, an important consideration here is that ERPP instruction, in any form or shape, needs to focus on both the writing and publishing aspect of scholarly publication. The current situation is that often the provision of ERPP support focuses on one or the other of these two aspects, depending on the expertise and the approach of the providers. As highlighted by Li and Flowerdew (2020), in many cases, ERPP provision deals only with the writing dimension of academic publication, focusing on discursive, rhetorical, and genre-specific properties of text. This approach leaves out "non-discursive" practices of academic publication (see Kwan, 2010), overlooking the fact that novice scholars "can turn out to have a rather vague understandings of the whole process of aca-demic publishing" (Delamont, Atkinson, & Parry, 2004, p. 174). What is missing in this approach is attention to non-discursive requirements and challenges.

With that in mind, a focused approach to the pedagogy of scholarly publi-cation requires that ERPP be among the concerns and on the priority list of course instructors and dissertation and thesis supervisors in different discip-lines. It is because they are among the very first frontline supporters that can play an important role in helping students to develop the necessary literacies. Course instructors and supervisors can orient their pedagogical practices and integrate their assignments with scholarly publication (Casanave, 2010). This will help novice scholars to converge their efforts in doing both the assignment and planning for future publications and will provide them with opportunities for feedback and support from their instructors and peers. However, the caveat here is that in today's neoliberal academy many graduate courses are taught by short-term contract faculty who themselves are novice scholars with no or limited experience in scholarly publication (Swales's [2019] speculation on the predicament of the typical EAP teacher confronted for the first time with teaching an ERPP course comes to mind here, see Chapter 9). Therefore, they themselves are also dealing with the challenges that their students are struggling with. Even if we accept that graduate courses should be taught by experienced instructors who are them-selves published scholars or that students should work under the mentorship of expert supervisors, as we indicated in Chapter 9, expertise in teaching disciplinary subjects or even being a published scholar does not guarantee expertise in teaching academic writing and publishing and the ability to share the expertise that comes with it. That is, often, established published scholars do not have the meta-language needed to explain how they do what they are doing. This highlights the fact that the provision of support for such elite practices as writing for scholarly publication requires expert ERPP specialists and experienced support providers. In the words of Paré (2010):

pedagogues who are engaged in that activity– that is, teachers who 'have learned the genres of their profession and are successful in them' – *and* [italics in the original] who are also able to induct students into their discipline's discourse practices.

p. 36

In addition to the role of course instructors and supervisors, ERPP services are currently provided mainly under the umbrella term of "EAP support". They are scattered across different schools and faculties in academic institutions and are offered mainly by writing support centres (or language/student support centres) across university campuses.

There is no doubt that the extent and quality of ERPP support provision varies across academic institutions in both Anglophone and (semi)peripheral academic contexts. However, there are a number of general issues and caveats that need attention regarding the current state of affairs. First, although EAP and ERPP expertise overlap to some extent, ERPP instruction requires further specialist knowledge, especially when it comes to the journal article genre and, more importantly, the publication phase of writing for scholarly publication. As Li and Flowerdew (2020, p. 38) argue, ERPP teacher education is "typically informal". Needless to say, many of the so-called writing specialists who work at writing centres are themselves graduate students who are serving their teaching assistantship (TA) or looking for a stipend to manage their graduate life. Consequently, they themselves are not necessarily trained as EAP (let alone ERPP) practitioners, and many of them have developed academic writing knowledge through trial and error. Furthermore, they are not necessarily experts in disciplinary discourses and genres and are not familiar with current scholarship in applied linguistics, EAP, ERPP, and language education. As discussed earlier, even if they are competent writers themselves, it does not necessarily make them academic writing instructors as efficient teaching requires both specialist knowledge as well as the meta-language to present that knowledge. Let alone the fact that many of them are themselves struggling with academic publishing and have no or limited experience in scholarly publication. This highlights the fact that "consideration of what is needed to be a successful ERPP teacher would be valuable" (Li & Flowerdew, 2020, p. 38) and underlines the significance of ERPP teacher training as one of the practical areas that deserves special attention at the institutional level.

Second, as the name suggests, writing centres are mainly focused on academic writing rather than scholarly publication or the publication aspect of academic writing per se. More importantly, their services are not necessarily structured and long term. They usually consist of short-term professional development opportunities such as one-day seminars, workshops, or short-term courses, as well as ad hoc, walk-in, or scheduled short conferences (meetings) with a writing specialist who provides feedback on a finished project and work in progress. Third, writing services offered at writing centres are generally geared towards undergraduate writing and assignments or graduate genres such as thesis and grant proposals. Last but not least, those services are more often geared towards the needs of EAL students, as there still exists "a strong perception that writing courses are remedial, so the courses are only for international students" (Fairbanks & Dias, 2016, p. 156). All these factors make the services provided at writing centres very limited in terms of variety and range, focusing mainly on editorial and cosmetic aspects of general academic writing and leaving out the RAs genre and its composition and dissemination processes.

It follows from the above that, in order to provide quality ERPP support, writing centres need to draw more on research-based and research-informed scholarship regarding ERPP pedagogy and mentorship. Also, they need to avoid undergraduate-centrism and expand their support to include graduate writing and scholarly pub-lication practices of novice scholars (Philips, 2013). Moreover, given that "writing centres have historically downplayed the need for tutors to be disciplinary experts" (Philips, 2016, p. 163), they need to use advisors and instructors who have both disciplinary and (meta)discursive expertise in the required academic genres and practices of scholarly publication (Habibie, 2019). Furthermore, they need to avoid advertising or offering their services in a way that creates a mentality that those services are merely targeted at EAL scholars, alienating Anglophone junior scholars who are also struggling with or interested in scholarly publication. In both adver-tising and providing ERPP support services, it is imperative to understand that "Anglophone junior scholars' affective and mental barriers in using such services are also a key consideration" (Habibie, 2019, p. 45).

In addition to the key role of course instructors and writing centres in pro-viding ERPP services, an ERPP course either provided by a specific department/faculty or writing centre is also a significant resource in supporting the devel-opment of required scholarly publication literacies. However, Li and Flowerdew (2020) suggest that "the provision of ERPP courses is perhaps still underdeveloped, especially as compared to, say, courses on undergraduate academic writing" (p. 38). They enumerate a number of reasons for limited provision of ERPP courses which relate to some of the aforementioned discussions. They include lack of awareness at the level of university administration of the significance of ERPP provision; lack of qualified educators to provide ERPP support and instruction; unwilling-ness on the part of EAP instructors to add ERPP instruction to their to-do list; the stigma towards undertaking ERPP training (see Flowerdew, 2008); lack of understanding on the part of supervisors and content instructors of the discursive and non-discursive challenges that junior scholars are facing for research communi-cation; logistical reasons such as lack of funding for designing and delivering ERPP education; and, last but not least, the attitude that ERPP socialisation comes natur-ally without any incidental intervention or training. As mentioned earlier, this pos-ition is very prevalent in many academic contexts and especially when it comes to Anglophone novice scholars. In other words, "[m]any stakeholders at both admin-istration and faculty levels still consider academic literacy in general and academic writing in particular as the Anglophone doctoral student's habitus (Bourdieu, 1977) and one of their innate dispositions" (Habibie, 2019, p. 43). That seems to be one of the reasons why "we still see little explicit teaching of writing at the graduate level" for Anglophone students in the Inner Circle academic context (Fairbanks & Dias, 2016, p. 140).

In conclusion, what is significant here is that ERPP awareness raising and support provision are key in current academia and require that different stakeholders engage and shoulder their responsibilities. There is no doubt that the implementation and success of institutional support interventions such as scholarly publication seminars, workshops, and writing centre services hinge upon a number of key factors and considerations. They require a meticulous coordination among departments, faculty members, and writing centres regarding the education of writing for scholarly publication (Habibie, 2019).

Looking to the future

In the final few paragraphs of this book, we will speculate on the future of ERPP and English as the language of international research and publication. An obvious aspect of ERPP that will develop in the future is that there will be increasing technological innovation in the publishing sphere. Following the COVID-19 pandemic, the demise of the print journal and academic book looks increasingly likely. This book was written across two continents during the pandemic lockdown. This was no impediment, however, as all of the resources needed in terms of journal articles and book chapters were available online via the libraries of the two authors or by means of interlibrary loan. Libraries will be increasingly hard-pressed to purchase print books and subscribe to print journals in the future. The benefits of this development apply to both publishers and academics. Publishing houses will no longer need to tie up capital in physical production facilities, product inventories, and distribution systems. Individual scholars will benefit from instant access to almost unlimited research resources. Whereas in the past, if a library did not subscribe to a particular journal or possess a particular book, an interlibrary loan could take weeks, now electronic formats of journal articles, books, and book chapters can be provided on-demand in the space of a day or two. Academics are, of course, benefitting from technological innovation in other ways, with more and more sophisticated social and other new media facilitating the exchange of information and construction of knowledge, at both the individual and the collaborative level (always allowing for unequal access to these resources), as outlined in Chapter 8. This can only increase. Although the commercial publishing houses are making their products more and more appealing, with innovations such as editing services and various online tools, the rise of the Open Access movement, as described in Chapter 8 again, is only likely to grow, with its more accessible, democratic, and financially attractive model having greater appeal on many fronts. We must also ask the question as to whether the increasing sophistication of artificial intelligence (AI) might at some point make writing in English for EAL writers no longer necessary, as the quality of translation will improve. Various studies have shown that many EAL writers are dissatisfied with the quality of translation when they have tried it and prefer to write in English, perhaps with the help of language assistance (e.g., St.

John, 1987). Their dissatisfaction stems from the problem of finding someone competent enough in both the English language and the discipline to be able to create an adequate translation. With ever-increasing computer power and sufficient "big data", the time may come when AI is capable of translating the most specialised of documents. This indeed is food for thought for ERPP.

Finally, what is in store for the English language itself? Will it maintain or even increase its dominance? Certainly, more and more countries are embracing the neoliberal model for their university systems and hence will encourage their academics to enter into the rankings and metrics game and seek to publish in English. Shchemeleva's (2021) recent account of this happening in one university in Russia is a good example on this front. Furthermore, as indicated in Chapter 3, as more and more EAL scholars seek to publish in English, there are signs that World Englishes and English as a Lingua Franca are gradually being accepted. As a counterweight to these arguments in support of the rising influence of English, some countries and regions are making efforts to promote the dissemination of knowledge in their own languages. France has long championed its language as a major research language and other Hispanophone countries are now also actively promoting more science publication in Spanish (Hyland, 2015). China too, which until recently was encouraging its scholars to publish internationally in SCI journals, including offering financial inducements, is now also promoting more publication in Chinese journals (Xu, 2020). More publication in the national language is also referred to by Shchemeleva (2021) for Russia. In spite of such promotion of local and regional languages, it is likely, however, that the desire for broader dissemination of knowledge and international recognition will outweigh any push for local or regional languages, except perhaps in the HSS and applied science disciplines.

In the longer term, a very important variable for the future of English is China. As indicated in Chapter 3, China produces more research papers in English than any other country, including the US. China's growing research output is commensurate with its increasing GDP. In 2020, China had a GDP of $14,860 billion, as compared to that of the US with a total GDP of $20,807 billion (Statista, 2020). It is likely that China will soon overtake the US, however, with a much higher economic growth rate (and a far lesser reduction in economic activity due to the COVID-19 pandemic). We have argued that the rise of English as the international language of research and publication has been due to economic power, on the one hand, and research output, on the other. This therefore raises the question as to whether Chinese might not at some point become a major language of international research and publication and pose a threat to the dominance of English. China is also making great efforts to extend its soft power, is in ideological conflict with the West, and the two political blocs are moving away from each other (Morrison, 2019). Could a similar parting of the ways happen in research and publication? Such an eventuality might seem remote, but given the factors we have set out, is certainly a possibility, especially if one considers that many of the university ranking tables are becoming populated with universities in East Asia. At the same time, though, one needs to consider India, another populous rising power, with

English as one of its official languages. Furthermore, it took English centuries to reach where it is now, albeit that any change in the balance of power might be more rapid now, due to technological advancement. Only time will tell the future, however. In the meantime, there is plenty for ERPP scholars and practitioners to be getting on with, as we hope to have shown in this book.

REFERENCES

Abramo, G., & D'Angelo, C. A. (2015). Evaluating university research: Same performance indicator, different rankings. *Journal of Informetrics, 9*(3), 514–525.

Ahmad, U. K. (1997). Research article introductions in Malay: Rhetoric in an emerging research community. In A. Duzak (Ed.), *Culture and styles of academic discourse* (pp. 273–304). Berlin: Mouton de Gruyter.

Aïssaoui, R., Geringer, J. M., & Livanis, G. (2021). International collaboration and European contributions to international business research. *Management International Review.* https://doi-org.ezproxy.lancs.ac.uk/10.1007/s11575-020-00435-6

Aitchison, C., & Guerin, C. (2014). Writing groups, pedagogy, theory and practice: An introduction. In C. Aitchison & C. Guerin (Eds.), *Writing groups for doctoral education and beyond* (pp. 27–54). Berlin: Routledge.

Ammon, U. (2000). Towards more fairness in international English: linguistic rights of non-native speakers? In R. Phillipson (Ed.), *Rights to language, equity and power in education* (pp. 111–116). Mahwah, NJ: Lawrence Erlbaum.

Ammon, U. (2001). Editor's preface. In U. Ammon (Ed.), *The dominance of English as a language of science* (pp. 5–10). Berlin: Mouton de Gruyter.

Ammon, U. (2007). Global scientific communication: Open questions and policy suggestions. In U. Ammon & A. Carli (Eds.), *Linguistic inequality in scientific communication today. AILA Review* [special issue], *20*, 123–133. Amsterdam: John Benjamins.

Ammon, U. (2016). English as a language of science. In A. Linn (Ed.), *Investigating English in Europe: Contexts and agendas* (pp. 34–39). Berlin: De Gruyter.

Anderson, B. (2006). *Imagined communities: Reflections on the origin and spread of nationalism.* London and New York: Verso.

Appadurai, A. (1990). Disjuncture and difference in the global cultural economy. *Theory, Culture & Society, 7*(2–3), 295–310.

Appadurai, A. (1996). *Modernity at large: Cultural dimensions of globalization.* Minneapolis, MN: University of Minnesota Press.

Atkinson, D. (1999). *Scientific discourse in sociohistorical context: The philosophical transactions of the royal society of London, 1675–1975.* Mahwah, NJ: Erlbaum.

Avula, J., & Avula, H. (2015). Authors, authorship order, the moving finger writes. *Journal of Indian Society of Periodontology, 19*(3), 258–262.

Bacon, F. (1848). Novum Organum (W. Wood, Trans.). In B. Montagu (Ed.), *The works of Francis Bacon, Lord Chancellor of England* (Vol. 3). Philadelphia, PA: Carey & Hart. (Original work published 1620).

Bajwa, N. H., & Konig, C. J. (2019). How much research in the top journals of industrial/organizational psychology dominated by authors from the US? *Scientometrics, 120*(3), 1147–1161.

Barber, C. L. (1962). Some measurable characteristics of modern scientific prose. *Contributions to English syntax and philology*, Gothenburg Studies in English, 14. Reprinted, with a commentary, in J. M. Swales (Ed.) (1988), *Episodes in ESP* (pp. 1–15). New York: Prentice-Hall.

Barton, D., & Hamilton, M. (1998). *Local literacies: Reading and writing in one community.* London: Routledge.

Basturkmen, H. (2012). A genre-based investigation of discussion sections of research articles in dentistry and disciplinary variation. *Journal of English for Academic Purposes, 11*(2), 134–144.

Bawarshi, A. S., & Reiff, M. J. (2010). *Genre: An introduction to history, theory, research, and pedagogy.* West Lafayette, IN: Parlor Press.

Bazerman, C. (1980). A relationship between reading and writing: The conversational model. *College English, 41*, 656–666.

Bazerman, C. (1988). *Shaping written knowledge: The genre and activity of the experimental article in science.* Madison, WI: University of Wisconsin Press.

Beall, J. (2010). "Predatory," open-access scholarly publishers. *The Charleston Advisor, 11*, 10–17.

Beall, J. (2012). Predatory publishers are corrupting open access. *Nature, 489*(7415), 179.

Beaufort, A. (2000). Learning the trade: A social apprenticeship model for gaining writing expertise. *Written Communication, 17*(2), 185–223.

Becher, T. (1989). *Academic tribes and territories: Intellectual enquiry and the cultures of disciplines.* Milton Keynes: The Society for Research into Higher Education & Open University Press.

Becher, T., & Trowler, P. R. (2001). *Academic tribes and territories: Intellectual enquiry and the cultures of disciplines* (2nd ed.). Buckingham: Open University Press.

Belcher, D. D. (2007). Seeking acceptance in an English-only research world. *Journal of Second Language Writing, 16*, 1–22.

Belcher, W. L. (2009). *Writing your journal article in 12 weeks: A guide to academic publishing success.* Thousand Oaks, CA: Sage.

Belikov, A. V., & Belikov, V. V. (2015). A citation-based, author- and age-normalized, logarithmic index for evaluation of individual researchers independently of publication counts [version 1; peer review: 2 approved]. *F1000Research, 4*.

Benesch, S. (2001). *Critical English for academic purposes: Theory, politics, and practice.* Mahwah, NJ: Lawrence Erlbaum.

Benfield, J., & Howard, K. (2000). The language of science. *European Journal of Cardio-Thoracic Surgery, 84*, 363–364.

Bennett, K. (2007). Epistemicide! The tale of a predatory discourse. *Translator, 13*, 151–169.

Bennett, K. (Ed.). (2014). *The semiperiphery of academic writing: Discourses, communities and practice.* London: Palgrave Macmillan.

Bennett, K. (2015). Towards an epistemological monoculture: Mechanisms of epistemicide in European research publication. In R. P. Alastrué & C. Pérez-Llantada (Eds.), *English as a scientific and research language: Debates and discourses* (pp. 9–36). Berlin, München, and Boston, MA: De Gruyter.

Benvenuti, S. (2017). Pedagogy of peers: Cultivating writing retreats as communities of academic writing practice. *South African Journal of Higher Education, 31*(2), 89–107.

Berkenkotter, C., & T. Huckin (1995). *Genre knowledge in disciplinary communication: Cognition/culture/power.* Hillsdale, NJ: Lawrence Erlbaum.

Bhatia, V. K. (1993). *Analysing genre: Language use in professional settings*. London: Longman.

Bhatia, V. K. (2004). *Worlds of written discourse: A genre-based view*. London: Continuum.

Bizzell, P. (1992). *Academic discourse and critical consciousness*. Pittsburgh, PA: University of Pittsburgh Press.

Björk, B. C., & Solomon, D. (2012). Open access versus subscription journals: A comparison of scientific impact. *BMC Medicine, 10*(1), 73.

Blackmore, P., & Kandiko, C. B. (2011). Motivation in academic life: A prestige economy. *Research in Post-Compulsory Education, 16*(4), 399–411.

Bocanegra-Valle, A. (2015). Peer reviewers' recommendations for language improvement in research writing. In R. Plo & C. Pérez-Llantada (Eds.), *English as a scientific and research language: Debates and discourses. English in Europe* (pp. 207–230). Berlin: De Gruyter.

Bodde, D. (1991). *Chinese thought, society, and science: The intellectual and social background of science and technology in pre-modern China*. Honolulu, HI: University of Hawaii Press.

Bordet, G. (2016). Counteracting domain loss and epistemicide in specialized discourse: A case study on the translation of anglophone metaphors to French. *Publications, 4*(2), 18. https://doi.org/10.3390/publications4020018

Bourdieu, P. (1977). The economics of linguistic exchanges. *Social Science Information, 16*(6), 645–668.

Bourdieu, P., Passeron, J. C., & Saint Martin, M. (1994). *Academic discourse: Linguistic misunderstanding and professorial power*. London: Polity.

Bowerman, M., & Levinson, S. C. (Eds.). (2001). *Language acquisition and conceptual development*. Cambridge: Cambridge University Press.

Breeze, R. (2015). Citing outside the community? An investigation of the language of bibliography in top journals. In R. P. Alastrué & C. Pérez-Llantada (Eds.), *English as a scientific and research language: Debates and discourses* (pp. 37–58). Berlin: De Gruyter.

Brown, R. (Ed.). (2011). *Higher education and the market*. New York and London: Routledge.

Brown, P., & Levinson, S. C. (1987). *Politeness: Some universals in language usage*. Cambridge,: Cambridge University Press.

Bruce, I. (2009). Results sections in sociology and organic chemistry articles: A genre analysis. *English for Specific Purposes, 28*(2), 105–124.

Brunner-Ried, J. J., & Salazar-Muñiz, F. (2012). Investigación educacional en Iberamérica: Entre la invisibilidad y la medición. *Magis Revista Internacional de Investigación en Educación, 4*(9), 559–575.

Bryant, A., & Charmaz, K. (2019). *The SAGE handbook of current developments in grounded theory*. Thousand Oaks, CA: Sage.

Buckingham, L. (2014). Building a career in English: Users of English as an additional language in academia in the Arabian Gulf. *TESOL Quarterly, 48*(1), 6–33.

Burgess, S., & Cargill, M. (2013). Using genre analysis and corpus linguistics to teach research article writing. In V. Matarese (Ed.), *Supporting research writing: Roles and challenges in multilingual settings* (pp. 55–71). Cambridge: Woodhead Publishing.

Burgess, S., Martín, P. A., & Balasanyan, D. (2019). English or Spanish for research publication purposes? Reflections on a critical pragmatic pedagogy. In J. N. Corcoran, K. Englander, & L.-M. Muresan (Eds.), *Pedagogies and policies for publishing research in English: Local initiatives supporting international scholars* (pp. 128–140). New York and London: Routledge.

Burrough-Boenisch, J. (2003). Shapers of published NNS research articles. *Journal of Second Language Writing, 12*, 223–243.

Cadman, K. (2017). Introducing research rigour in the social sciences. In M. Cargill & S. Burgess (Eds.), *Publishing research in English as an additional language* (pp. 33–54). Adelaide: University of Adelaide Press.

Cameron, C., Deming, S. P., Notzon, B., Cantor, S. B., Broglio, K. R., & Pagel, W. (2009). Scientific writing training for academic physicians of diverse language backgrounds. *Academic Medicine, 84*(4), 505–510.

Canagarajah, A. S. (1996). "Nondiscursive" requirements in academic publishing, material resources of periphery scholars, and the politics of knowledge production. *Written Communication, 13*(4), 435–472.

Canagarajah, A. S. (2002). *A geopolitics of academic writing.* Pittsburgh, PA: University of Pittsburgh Press.

Canagarajah, S. (2018). English as a spatial resource and the claimed competence of Chinese STEM professionals. *World Englishes, 37,* 34–50.

Cargill, M., & Burgess, S. (2008). Introduction to the special issue: English for research publication purposes. *Journal of English for Academic Purposes, 7*(2), 75–76.

Cargill, M., & O'Connor, P. (2006). Developing Chinese scientists' skills for publishing in English: Evaluating collaborating-colleague workshops based on genre analysis. *Journal of English for Academic Purposes, 5*(3), 207–221.

Cargill, M., & O'Connor, P. (2013). *Writing scientific research articles: Strategy and steps.* Oxford: Wiley-Blackwell.

Cargill, M., & Smernik, R. (2016). Embedding publication skills in science research training: A writing group program based on applied linguistics frameworks and facilitated by a scientist. *Higher Education Research and Development, 35*(2), 229–241.

Carter, S., & Laurs, D. (Eds.). (2017). *Developing research writing: A handbook for supervisors and advisors* (1st ed.). London: Routledge.

Casanave, C. P. (1998). Transitions: The balancing act of bilingual academics. *Journal of Second Language Writing, 12,* 175–203.

Casanave, C. P. (2002). *Writing games: Multicultural case studies of academic literacy practices in higher education.* Mahwah, NJ: Lawrence Erlbaum.

Casanave, C. P. (2010). Dovetailing under impossible circumstances. In C. Aitchison, B. Kamler, & A. Lee (Eds.), *Publishing pedagogies for the doctorate and beyond* (pp. 83–101). New York: Routledge.

Casanave, C. P. (2019). Does writing for publication ever get easier? Some reflections from an experienced scholar. In P. Habibie & K. Hyland (Eds.), *Novice writers and scholarly publication: Authors, mentors, gatekeepers* (pp. 135–151). Cham, Switzerland: Palgrave Macmillan.

Casanave, C. P., & Vandrick, S. (Eds.). (2003). *Writing for scholarly publication: Behind the scenes in language education.* Mahwah, NJ: Erlbaum.

Catterall, J., Ross, P., Aitchison, C., & Burgin, S. (2011). Pedagogical approaches that facilitate writing in postgraduate research candidature in science and technology. *Journal of University Teaching and Learning Practice, 8*(2), 2–10.

Charles, M. (2014). Getting the corpus habit: EAP students' long-term use of personal corpora. *English for Specific Purposes, 35,* 30–40.

Charles, M. (2015). Same task, different corpus: The role of personal corpora in EAP classes. In A. Lenko-Szymanska & A. Boulton (Eds.), *Multiple affordances of language corpora for data-driven learning* (pp. 129–154). Amsterdam and Philadelphia, PA: John Benjamins.

Chen, M., & Flowerdew, J. (2018). A critical review of research and practice in data-driven learning (DDL) in the academic writing classroom. *International Journal of Corpus Linguistics, 23*(3), 335–369.

Cheng, A. (2018). *Genre and graduate-level research writing.* Ann Arbor, MI: University of Michigan Press.

Cheung, Y. L. (2010). First publications in refereed English journals: Difficulties, coping strategies, and recommendations for student training. *System, 38*(1), 134–141.

Chinchilla-Rodriguez, Z., Miao, L., Murray, D., Robinson-Garcia, N., Costas, R., & Sugimoto, C. R. (2018). A global comparison of scientific mobility and collaboration according to national scientific capacities. *Frontiers in Research Metrics and Analytics, 3*(17), 1–14.

Cho, S. (2004). Challenges of entering discourse communities through publishing in English: Perspectives of nonnative-speaking doctoral students in the United States of America. *Journal of Language, Identity & Education, 3*(1), 47–72.

Clandinin, D., & Connelly, F. (2000). *Narrative inquiry: Experience and story in qualitative research* (1st ed.). San Francisco, CA: Jossey-Bass Publishers.

Clarivate Analytics (2020). The repository selection process. Retrieved from https://clarivate.com/webofsciencegroup/essays/the-repository-selection-process/

Clavero, M. (2010). "Awkward wording. Rephrase": Linguistic injustice in ecological journals. *Trends in Ecology & Evolution, 25*(10), 552–553.

Coniam, D. (2012). Exploring reviewer reactions to papers submitted to academic journals. *System, 40*, 544–553.

Connor, U. (1998). Comparing research and not-for-profit grant proposals. In U. Connor (Ed.), *Written discourse in philanthropic fundraising: Issues of language and rhetoric* (pp. 45–64). Indianapolis, IN: Indiana Center on Philanthropy.

Connor, U. (2000). Variations in rhetorical moves in grant proposals of US humanists and scientists. *Text, 20*, 1–28.

Connor, U. (2011). *Intercultural rhetoric in the writing classroom.* Ann Arbor, MI: University of Michigan Press.

Connor, U., & Mauranen, A. (1999). Linguistic analysis of grant proposals: European Union research grants. *English for Specific Purposes, 18*, 47–62.

Connor, U., & Upton, T. A. (2004). The genre of grant proposals: A corpus linguistic analysis. In U. Connor & T. Upton (Eds.), *Discourse in the professions: Perspectives from corpus linguistics.* (pp. 235–255). Amsterdam: John Benjamins Publishing Company.

Connor, U., & Wagner, L. (1999). Language use in grant proposals by nonprofits: Spanish and English. *New Directions for Philanthropic Fundraising, 22*, 59–73.

Coolidge, A. C. (1932). *Archibald Cary Coolidge: Life and letters.* Boston, MA: Houghton Mifflin Company.

Corcoran, J. (2019). Addressing the "bias gap": A research-driven argument for critical support of plurilingual scientists' research writing. *Written Communication, 36*(4), 538–577.

Corcoran, J., & Englander, K. (2016). A proposal for critical-pragmatic pedagogical approaches to English for research publication purposes. *Publications, 4*(6), 1–10.

Corcoran, J., Englander, K., & Muresan, L. (Eds.). (2019). *Pedagogies and policies for publishing research in English: Local initiatives supporting international scholars.* New York: Routledge.

Cortes, V. (2013). "The purpose of this study is to": Connecting lexical bundles and moves in research article introductions. *Journal of English for Academic Purposes, 12*, 33–43.

Cotos, E. (2019). Articulating societal benefits in grant proposals: Move analysis of Broader Impacts. *English for Specific Purposes, 54*, 15–34.

Cotos, E., Huffman, S., & Link, S. (2015). Furthering and applying move/step constructs: Technology-driven marshalling of Swalesian genre theory for EAP pedagogy. *Journal of English for Academic Purposes, 19*, 52–72.

Cotos, E., Huffman, S., & Link, S. (2017). A move/step model for Methods sections: Demonstrating rigour and credibility. *English for Specific Purposes, 46*, 90–106.

Cotos, E., Link, S., & Huffman, S. (2017). Effects of DDL technology on genre learning. *Language, Learning and Technology, 21*(3), 104–130.

Crystal, D. (2003). *English as a global language* (2nd ed.). Cambridge: Cambridge University Press.

Curry, J. M., & Lillis, T. (2004). Multilingual scholars and the imperative to publish in English: Negotiating interests, demands, and rewards. *TESOL Quarterly, 38*(3), 663–688.

Curry, M. J., & Lillis, T. (2013). *A scholar's guide to getting published in English: Critical choices and practical strategies.* Bristol: Multilingual Matters.

Darvin, R., & Norton, B. (2019). Collaborative writing, academic socialization, and the negotiation of identity. In P. Habibie & K. Hyland (Eds.), *Novice writers and scholarly publication: Authors, mentors, gatekeepers* (pp. 177–194). Cham, Switzerland: Palgrave Macmillan.

Davies, A. (2006). The native speaker in applied linguistics. In A. Davies & C. Elder (Eds.), *The handbook of applied linguistics* (pp. 431–450). Oxford: Blackwell.

Davis, K. A. (1994). Qualitative theory and methods in applied linguistics research. *TESOL Quarterly, 29*(3), 427–453.

Davis, P., & Walters, W. (2011). The impact of free access to the scientific literature: A review of recent research (EC). *Journal of the Medical Library Association, 99*(3), 208–217.

Day, R. A. (1989). The origins of the scientific paper: The IMRAD format. *AMWA Journal, 4*, 16–18.

Day, R. A., & Gastel, B. (2006). *How to write and publish a scientific paper* (6th ed.). Westport, CN: Greenwood Press.

de Swaan, A. (2001a). *Words of the world: The global language system.* Cambridge: Polity.

de Swaan, A. (2001b). English in social sciences. In U. Ammon (Ed.), *The dominance of English as a language of science: Effects on other languages and language communities* (pp. 71–82). Berlin: De Gruyter, Inc.

Delamont, S., Atkinson, P., & Parry, O. (2004). *Supervising the doctorate: A guide to success.* London: Open University Press.

Di Bitetti, M. S., & Ferreras, J. A. (2017). Publish (in English) or perish: The effect on citation rate of using languages other than English in scientific publications. *Ambio, 46*(1), 121–127.

DiGiacomo, S. M. (2013). Giving authors a voice in another language through translation. In V. Matarese (Ed.), *Supporting research writing: Roles and challenges in multilingual settings* (pp. 107–120). Oxford: Chandos Publishing.

Dong, J., & Liu, X. (2020). Promoting discipline-specific genre competence with corpus-based genre analysis activities. *English for Specific Purposes, 58*, 138–154.

Drayton, E., & Waltmann, B. (2020). Will universities need a bailout to survive the COVID-19 crisis? Institute of Fiscal Studies Briefing Note. Retrieved from www.ifs.org.uk/uploads/BN300-Will-universities-need-bailout-survive-COVID-19-crisis-1.pdf

Driscoll, A., & Driscoll, J. (2002). Writing an article for publication: An open invitation. *Journal of Orthopaedic Nursing, 6*(3), 144–152.

Dubois, B. L. (1980a). Genre and structure of biomedical speeches. *Forum Linguisticum, 5*, 140–168.

Dubois, B. (1980b). The use of slides in biomedical speeches. *The ESP Journal, 1*, 45–50.

Duff, P. A. (2010). Language socialization into academic discourse communities. *Annual Review of Applied Linguistics, 30*, 169–192.

Duszak, A., & Lewkowicz, J. (2008). Publishing academic texts in English: A Polish perspective. *Journal of English for Academic Purposes, 7*, 108–120.

Eberhard, D. M., Simons, G. F., & Fennig, C. D. (Eds.). (2020). *Ethnologue: Languages of the world.* (23rd ed.). Dallas, TX: SIL International.

Ellis, R. (2003). *Task-based language teaching and learning.* Oxford: Oxford University Press.

Elola, I., & Oskoz, A. (2017). Writing with 21st century social tools in the L2 classroom: New literacies, genres, and writing practices. *Journal of Second Language Writing, 36*, 52–60.

Englander, K. (2009). Transformation of the identities of nonnative English-speaking scientists as a consequence of the social construction of revision. *Journal of Language, Identity & Education, 8*(1), 35–53.

Englander, K. (2014). *Writing and publishing science research papers in English: A global perspective.* New York: Springer.

Englander, K., & Corcoran, J. (2019). *English for research publication purposes: Critical plurilingual pedagogies.* New York: Routledge.

Englander, K., & López-Bonilla, G. (2011). Acknowledging or denying membership: Reviewers' responses to non-anglophone scientists' manuscripts. *Discourse Studies, 13,* 395–416.

Erasmus + (2021). Retrieved from https://ec.europa.eu/programmes/erasmus-plus/node_en

Eriksson, A. (2012). Pedagogical perspectives on bundles: Teaching bundles to doctoral students of biochemistry. In J. Thomas & A. Boulton (Eds.), *Input, process and product: Developments in teaching and language corpora* (pp. 195–211). Brno, Czech Republic: Masaryk University Press.

Fairbanks, K., & Dias, S. (2016). Going beyond L2 graduate writing: Redesigning an ESL program to meet the needs of both L2 and L1 graduate students. In S. Simpson et al. (Eds.), *Supporting graduate student writers* (pp. 139–158). Ann Arbor, MI: University of Michigan Press.

Fazel, I. (2019). Writing for publication as a native speaker: The experiences of two anglophone novice scholars. In P. Habibie & K. Hyland (Eds.), *Novice writers and scholarly publication: Authors, mentors, gatekeepers* (pp. 79–95). London: Palgrave Macmillan.

Feak, C. B., & Swales, J. (2010). Writing for publication: Corpus-informed materials for postdoctoral fellows in perinatology. In N. Harwood (Ed.), *English language teaching materials: Theory and practice* (pp. 279–300). Cambridge: Cambridge University Press.

Feng, H., & Shi, L. (2004). Genre analysis of research grant proposals. *LSP & Professional Communication, 4*(1), 8–30.

Feng, H., Beckett, G. H., & Huang, D. (2013). From 'import' to 'import-export' oriented on scholarly publication in China. *Language Policy, 12,* 251–272.

Ferenz, O. (2005). EFL writers' social networks: Impact on advanced academic literacy development. *Journal of English for Academic Purposes, 4*(4), 339–351.

Ferguson, G. (1997). Teacher education and LSP: The role of specialized knowledge. In R. Howard & G. Brown (Eds.), *Teacher education for languages for specific purposes* (pp. 80–89). Clevedon: Multilingual Matters.

Ferguson, G. (2007). The global spread of English, scientific communication and ESP: Questions of equity, access and domain loss. *Ibérica, 13,* 7–38.

Ferguson, G., Pérez-Llantada, C., & Plo, R. (2011). English as an international language of scientific publication: A study of attitudes. *World Englishes, 30,* 41–59.

Flowerdew, J. (1993). An educational, or process, approach to the teaching of professional genres. *ELT Journal, 47,* 305–316.

Flowerdew, J. (1999a). Writing for scholarly publication in English: The case of Hong Kong. *Journal of Second Language Writing, 8*(2), 123–145.

Flowerdew, J. (1999b). Problems in writing for scholarly publication in English: The case of Hong Kong. *Journal of Second Language Writing, 8*(3), 243–264.

Flowerdew, J. (2000). Discourse community, legitimate peripheral participation, and the nonnative-English-speaking scholar. *TESOL Quarterly, 34*(1), 127–150.

Flowerdew, J. (2001). Attitudes of journal editors to non-native speaker contributions. *TESOL Quarterly, 35*(1), 121–150.

Flowerdew, J. (Ed.) (2002). *Academic discourse.* London: Longman.

Flowerdew, J. (2007). The non-Anglophone scholar on the periphery of scholarly publication. *AILA Review, 20*, 14–27.

Flowerdew, J. (2008). Scholarly writers who use English as an additional language: What can Goffman's "Stigma" tell us? *Journal of English for Academic Purposes, 7*(2), 77–86.

Flowerdew, J. (2011). Reconciling approaches to genre analysis in ESP: The whole can equal more than the sum of the parts. In D. Belcher, A. Johns, & B. Paltridge (Eds.), *New directions in ESP research* (pp. 119–144). Ann Arbor, MI: University of Michigan Press.

Flowerdew, J. (2013a). English for research publication purposes. In B. Paltridge & S. Starfield (Eds.), *The handbook of English for specific purposes* (pp. 301–321). Oxford: Wiley/Blackwell.

Flowerdew, J. (2013b). *Discourse in English language education*. London: Routledge.

Flowerdew, J. (2015). Some thoughts on English for Research Publication Purposes (ERPP) and related issues. *Language Teaching, 46*, 1–13.

Flowerdew, J. (2019). The linguistic disadvantage of scholars who write in English as an additional language: Myth or reality. *Language Teaching, 52*(2), 249–260.

Flowerdew, J., & Dudley-Evans, T. (2002). Genre analysis of editorial letters to international journal contributors. *Applied Linguistics, 23*, 463–489.

Flowerdew, J., & Li, Y. (2007). Language re-use among Chinese apprentice scientists writing for publication. *Applied Linguistics, 28*(3), 440–465.

Flowerdew, J., & Li, Y. (2009). English or Chinese? The trade-off between local and international publication among Chinese academics in the humanities and social sciences. *Journal of Second Language Writing, 18*(1), 17–29.

Flowerdew, J., & Wang, S. H. (2015). Identity in academic discourse. *Annual Review of Applied Linguistics, 35*, 81–99.

Flowerdew, J., & Wang, S. H. (2017). Teaching English for research publication purposes with a focus on register, genre, textual mentors and language re-use. In J. Flowerdew & T. Costley (Eds.), *Discipline-specific writing: Theory into practice* (pp. 144–161). London and New York: Routledge.

Flowerdew, L. (2016). A genre-inspired and lexico-grammatical approach for helping postgraduate students craft research grant proposals. *English for Specific Purposes, 42*, 1–12.

Fortanet, I. (2008). Evaluative language in peer review referee reports. *Journal of English for Academic Purposes, 7*(1), 27–37.

Foucault, M. (1980). Truth and power. In C. Gordon (Ed.), *Power/knowledge: Selected interviews and other writings 1972–1977* (pp. 109–133). Brighton: Harvester Press.

Freda, M., & Kearney, M. (2005). An international survey of nurse editors' roles and practices. *Journal of Nursing Scholarship, 37*(1), 87–94.

Fry, H., Kettering, S., & Marshall, S. (Eds.). (2008). *A handbook for teaching and learning in higher education*. London: Routledge.

Gann, L. (2020). What is considered a good impact factor? Retrieved from https://mdanderson.libanswers.com/faq/26159

Geertz, C. (1983). *Local knowledge: Further essays in interpretive anthropology*. New York: Basic Books.

Gentil, G., & Séror, J. (2014). Canada has two official languages—Or does it? Case studies of Canadian scholars' language choices and practices in disseminating knowledge. *Journal of English for Academic Purposes, 13*(1), 17–30.

Gerber, L. G. (2014). *The rise and decline of faculty governance: Professionalization and the modern American university*. Baltimore, MD: Johns Hopkins University Press.

Gibbs, W. W. (1995). Lost science in the Third World. *Scientific American*, August 1, 76–83.

Giddens, A. (1990). *The consequences of modernity*. Cambridge: Polity Press.

Gillaerts, P., & Van de Velde, F. (2010). Interactional metadiscourse in research article abstracts. *Journal of English for Academic Purposes, 9*(2), 128–139.

Gil-Salom, L., & Soler-Monreal, C. (2009). Interacting with the reader: Politeness in engineering research article discussions. *International Journal of English Studies, 9*(3), 175–190.

Glasman-Deal, H. (2010). *Science research writing for non-native speakers of English.* Singapore: World Scientific Publishing Pte.

Gnutzmann, C., & Rabe, F. (2014). "Theoretical subtleties" or "text modules"? German researchers' language demands and attitudes across disciplinary cultures. *Journal of English for Academic Purposes, 13*, 31–40.

Gonzalez, C. (2004). The role of blended learning in the world of technology. Retrieved December 10, 2004 from www.unt.edu/benchmarks/archives/2004/september04/eis. htm

Gosden, H. (1996). Verbal reports of Japanese novices' research writing practices in English. *Journal of Second Language Writing, 5*, 109–128.

Gosden, H. (2003). "Why not give us the full story?": Functions of referees' comments in peer reviews of scientific research papers. *Journal of English for Academic Purposes, 2*(2), 87–101.

Graves, H., Moghaddasi, S., & Hashim, A. (2013). Mathematics is the method: Exploring the macro-organizational structure of research articles in mathematics. *Discourse Studies, 15*(4), 421–438.

Guardiano, C., Favilla, M. E., & Calaresu, E. (2007). Stereotypes about English as the language of science. *AILA Review, 20*, 28–52.

Guerin, C., & Aitchison, C. (2017). Peer writing groups. In S. Carter & D. Laurs (Eds.), *Developing research writing* (1st ed., Vol. 1; pp. 51–55). London: Routledge.

Gunnarsson, B. (2011). *Languages of science in the eighteenth century.* Berlin and New York: De Gruyter Mouton.

Habibie, P. (2015). *An investigation into writing for scholarly publication by novice scholars: Practices of Canadian Anglophone doctoral students.* Unpublished doctoral dissertation. The University of Western Ontario, Canada.

Habibie, P. (2016). Writing for scholarly publication in a Canadian higher education context: A case study. In C. M. Badenhorst & C. Guerin (Eds.), *Research literacies and writing pedagogies for masters and doctoral writers* (pp. 51–67). Studies in writing series. Leiden: Brill Publishing.

Habibie, P. (2019). To be native or not to be native: That is not the question. In P. Habibie & K. Hyland (Eds.), *Novice writers and scholarly publication: Authors, mentors, gatekeepers* (pp. 35–52). Cham, Switzerland: Palgrave Macmillan.

Habibie, P., & Burgess, S. (Eds.). (forthcoming). *Scholarly publication trajectories of early-career scholars: Insider perspectives.* Palgrave Macmillan.

Habibie, P., & Hultgren, A. K. (Eds.). (forthcoming). *The inner world of gatekeeping in scholarly publication.* Palgrave Macmillan.

Habibie, P., & Hyland, K. (Eds.) (2019). *Novice writers and scholarly publication: Authors, mentors, gatekeepers.* Cham, Switzerland: Palgrave Macmillan.

Hafner, C. A. (2018). Genre innovation and multimodal expression in scholarly communication: Video methods articles in experimental biology. *Ibérica, 36*, 15–41.

Hafner, C. A., & Pun, J. (2020). Editorial: Introduction to this Special Issue: English for Academic and Professional Purposes in the Digital Era. *RELC Journal, 51*(1), 3–13.

Halliday, M. A. K. (2004). *The language of science.* (Collected Works of M. A. K. Halliday, Vol. 5, J. Webster [Ed.]). London and New York: Continuum International Publishing.

Hamel, R. E. (2007). The dominance of English in the international scientific periodical literature. *AILA Review, 20*, 53–71.

Hanauer, D. I., Sheridan, C. L., & Englander, K. (2019). Linguistic injustice in the writing of research articles in English as a second language: Data from Taiwanese and Mexican researchers. *Written Communication, 36*, 136–154.

Happell, B. (2011). Responding to reviewers' comments as part of writing for publication. *Nurse Researcher, 18*(4), 23–27.

Harvey, D. (2005). *A brief history of neoliberalism*. Oxford: Oxford University Press.

Harwood, N., & Hadley, G. (2004). Demystifying institutional practices: Critical pragmatism and the teaching academic writing. *English for Specific Purposes, 21*(4), 355–377.

Harwood, N., Austin, L., & Macaulay, R. (2009). Proofreading in a UK university: Proofreaders' beliefs, practices, and experiences. *Journal of Second Language Writing, 18*, 166–190.

Hasrati, M. (2005). Legitimate peripheral participation and supervising Ph.D. students. *Studies in Higher Education, 30*(5), 557–570.

Heard, S. B. (2016). *The scientist's guide to writing: How to write more easily and effectively throughout your scientific career*. Princeton, NJ: Princeton University Press.

Hewings, M. (2004). An important contribution or tiresome reading? A study of evaluation in peer reviews of journal article submissions. *Journal of Applied Linguistics, 1*(3), 247–274.

Hewings, A., Lillis, T., & Vladimirou, D. (2010). Who's citing whose writings? A corpus-based study of citations as interpersonal resource in English medium national and English medium international journals. *Journal of English for Academic Purposes, 9*, 102–115.

Hirano, E. (2009). Research article introductions in English for Specific purposes: A comparison between Brazilian Portuguese and English. *English for Specific Purposes, 28*, 240–250.

Hirsch, J. E. (2005). An index to quantify an individual's scientific research output. *Proceedings of the National Academy of Sciences, 102*(46), 16569–16572.

Holliday, A. (2005). *The struggle to teach English as an international language*. Oxford: Oxford University Press.

Hook, S., & Forey, G. (2005). Introducing a conference paper: Getting interpersonal with your audience. *Journal of English for Academic Purposes, 4*, 291–306.

Horn, S. A. (2017). Non-English nativeness as stigma in academic settings. *Academy of Management Learning and Education, 16*(4), 579–602.

Hu, G., & Cao, F. (2011). Hedging and boosting in abstracts of applied linguistics articles: A comparative study of English- and Chinese-medium journals. *Journal of Pragmatics, 43*(11), 2795–2809.

Huang, Ju C. (2010). Publishing and learning writing for publication in English: Perspectives of NNES PhD students in science. *Journal of English for Academic Purposes, 9*(1), 33–44.

Huddleston, R. D. (1971). *The sentence in written English: A syntactic study based on an analysis of scientific texts*. Cambridge: Cambridge University Press.

Hultgren, A. K. (2019). English as the language for academic publication: On equity, disadvantage and 'non-nativeness' as a red herring. *Publications, 7*(2), 31.

Hultgren, A. K., & Habibie, P. (Eds.). (forthcoming). *Women in scholarly publishing*. London: Routledge.

Hyland, K. (1998a). Persuasion and context: The pragmatics of academic metadiscourse. *Journal of Pragmatics, 30*(4), 437–455.

Hyland, K. (1998b). Boosting, hedging and the negotiation of academic knowledge. *Text, 18*(3), 349–382.

Hyland, K. (2000/2004). *Disciplinary discourses: Social interactions in academic writing*. London: Longman; Ann Arbor, MI: University of Michigan Press.

Hyland, K. (2007). Genre pedagogy: Language, literacy and L2 writing instruction. *Journal of Second Language Writing, 16*(3), 148–164.

Hyland, K. (2009). *Academic discourse*. London: Continuum.

Hyland, K. (2012). *Disciplinary identities: Individuality and community in academic discourse.* Cambridge: Cambridge University Press.

Hyland, K. (2015). *Academic publishing: Issues and challenges in the construction of knowledge.* Oxford, UK: Oxford University Press.

Hyland, K. (2016). Academic publishing and the myth of linguistic injustice. *Journal of Second Language Writing, 31,* 58–69.

Hyland, K. (2020). Peer review: Objective screening or wishful thinking. *Journal of English for Research Publication Purposes, 1*(1), 51–65.

Hymes, D. H. (1974). *Foundations in sociolinguistics: An ethnographic approach.* Philadelphia, PA: University of Pennsylvania Press.

Hynninen, N. (2020). Moments and mechanisms of intervention along textual trajectories: Norm negotiations in English-medium research writing. *Text & Talk,* October 29.

Hynninen, N., & Kuteeva, M. (2017). 'Good' and 'acceptable' English in L2 research writing: Ideals and realities in history and computer science. *Journal of English for Academic Purposes, 30,* 53–65.

Ives, P. (2006). Global English: Linguistic imperialism or practical lingua franca? *Studies in Language and Capitalism, 1,* 121–141.

Jack, A. (2017, March 15). Government targets sharp growth in foreign student numbers. *Financial Times,* p. 11.

Jenkins, J. (2011). Accommodating (to) ELF in the international university. *Journal of Pragmatics, 43,* 926–936.

Jenkins, J., Baker, W., & Dewey, M. (Eds.). (2018). *The Routledge handbook of English as a lingua franca.* London: Routledge.

Jogthong, C. (2001). *Research article introductions in Thai. Genre analysis of academic writing.* Unpublished doctoral dissertation. West Virginia University, Morgantown.

Johns, T. (1991). Should you be persuaded: Two examples of data-driven learning. *ELR Journal, 4,* 1–16.

Johnson, R., Watkinson, A., & Mabe, M. (2018). *The STM report: An overview of scientific and scholarly publishing* (5th ed.). The Hague, the Netherlands: International Association of Scientific, Technical and Medical Publishers.

Kachru, B. B. (1985). Institutionalized second-language varieties. In S. Greenbaum (Ed.), *The English language today* (pp. 211–226). Oxford: Pergamon.

Kachru, B. B. (1992). The second diaspora of English. In T. W. Machan & C. T. Scott (Eds.), *English in its social contexts: Essays in historical sociolinguistics* (pp. 230–252). Oxford: Oxford University Press.

Kachru, B. B., Kachru, Y., & Nelson, C. L. (Eds.). (2006/2009). *The handbook of world Englishes.* Oxford: Wiley-Blackwell.

Kamler, B., & Thomson, P. (2006). *Helping doctoral students write: Pedagogies for supervision.* New York, NY and London: Routledge.

Kaplan, R. B. (2001). English — the accidental language of science. In U. Ammon (Ed.), *The dominance of English as a language of science: Effects on other languages and language communities* (pp. 3–26). Berlin: De Gruyter, Inc.

Kapp, C. A., Albertyn, R. M., & Frick, B. L. (2011). Writing for publication: An intervention to overcome barriers to scholarly writing. *South African Journal of Higher Education, 25*(4), 741–759.

Keen, A. (2007). Writing for publication: Pressures, barriers and support strategies. *Nurse Education Today, 27*(5), 382–388.

Khadilkar, S. S. (2018). Rejection blues: Why do research papers get rejected? *Journal of Obstetrics and Gynecology India, 68,* 239–241.

Khadka, S. (2014). Geopolitics of grant writing: Discursive and stylistic features of non-profit grant proposals in Nepal and the United States. *Journal of Technical Writing and Communication, 44*(2), 141–170.

Kiley, M. (2009). Identifying threshold concepts and proposing strategies to support doctoral candidates. *Innovations in Education and Teaching International, 46*(3): 293–304.

Kirkpatrick, A. (2010). *The Routledge handbook of world Englishes.* Abingdon: Routledge.

Köhler, T., González-Morales, M. G., Banks, G. C., O'Boyle, E., Allen, J. A., Sinha, R., & Gulick, L. M.V. (2020). Supporting robust, rigorous, and reliable reviewing as the cornerstone of our profession: Introducing a competency framework for peer review. *Industrial and Organizational Psychology: Perspectives on Science and Practice, 13*(1), 1–27.

Kolata, G. (2017, October 30). Many academics are eager to publish in worthless journals. *The New York Times.* Retrieved from www.nytimes.com/2017/10/30/science/predatory-journals-academics.html

König, C., & Bajwa, N. (2020). In our English-only research world, there is a need for reviewers who are tolerant of imperfect texts from non-anglophone authors. *Industrial and Organizational Psychology, 13*(1), 54–56.

Kourilova, M. (1996). Interactive function of language in peer review of medical papers written by NN users of English. *UNESCO-ALSED LSP Newsletter, 19*, 4–21.

Kress, G. (2010). *Multimodality: A social semiotic approach to contemporary communication.* New York: Routledge.

Kronick, D. (1976). *A history of scientific and technical periodicals: The origins and development of the scientific and technical press 1665–1790* (2nd ed.). Metuchen, NJ: Scarecrow.

Kuteeva, M., & Mauranen, A. (2018). Digital academic discourse: texts and contexts: Introduction. *Discourse, Context & Media, 24*, 1–7.

Kwan, B. (2010). An investigation of instruction in research publishing offered in doctoral programs: The Hong Kong case. *Higher Education, 59*, 55–68.

Kwan, B. (2013). Facilitating novice researchers in project publishing during the doctoral years and beyond: A Hong Kong-based study. *Studies in Higher Education, 38*(2), 207–225.

La Madeleine, B. L. (2007). Lost in translation. *Nature (London), 445*(7126), 454–455.

Langum, V., & Kirk Sullivan, P. H. (2017). Writing academic English as a doctoral student in Sweden: Narrative perspectives, *Journal of Second Language Writing, 35*, 20–25.

Larson, B. P., & Chung, K. C. (2012). A systematic review of peer review for scientific manuscripts. *Hand (New York), 7*(1), 37–44.

Lash, S., & Urry, J. (1987). *The end of organized capitalism.* Madison, WI: University of Wisconsin Press.

Latour, B., & Woolgar, S. (1986). *Laboratory life: The construction of scientific facts.* Princeton, NJ: Princeton University Press.

Laurén, C. (2002). The conflict between national languages and English as the languages of arts and sciences. In G. Cortese & P. Riley (Eds.), *Domain-specific English* (pp. 87–97). Bern, Switzerland: Peter Lang.

Lave, J., & Wenger, E. (1991). *Situated learning: Legitimate peripheral participation.* Cambridge and New York: Cambridge University Press.

Le, T., & Harrington, M. (2015). Phraseology used to comment on results in the Discussion section of applied linguistics quantitative research articles. *English for Specific Purposes, 39*, 45–61.

Lea, M. R. (2015). Academic literacies in theory and practice. In B. Street & S. May (Eds.), *Literacies and language education. Encyclopedia of language and education* (3rd ed., pp. 1–12). Cham, Switzerland: Springer.

Lea, M. R., & Street, B.V. (2006). The "academic literacies" model: Theory and applications. *Theory into Practice, 45*(4), 368–377.

Lee, A., & Kamler, B. (2008). Bringing pedagogy to doctoral publishing. *Teaching in Higher Education, 13*(5), 511–523.

Lee, C. J., Sugimoto, C., Freeman, G. Z., & Cronin, B. (2013). Bias in peer review (Report). *Journal of the American Society for Information Science and Technology, 64*(1), 2–17.

Lee, D., & Swales, J. (2006). A corpus-based EAP course for NNS doctoral students: Moving from available specialized corpora to self-compiled corpora. *English for Specific Purposes, 25*(1), 56–75.

Lee, H., & Lee, K. (2013). Publish (in international indexed journals) or perish: Neoliberal ideology in a Korean university. *Language Policy, 12*(3), 215–230.

Leki, I. (2003). Tangled webs: Complexities of professional writing. In C. P. Casanave & S. Vandrick (Eds.), *Writing for scholarly publication: Behind the scenes in language education* (pp. 103–112). Mahwah, NJ: Lawrence Erlbaum Associates.

Li, Y. (2002). Writing for international publication: The perception of Chinese doctoral researchers. *Asian Journal of English Language Teaching, 12*, 179–194.

Li, Y. (2005). Multidimensional enculturation: The case of an EFL Chinese doctoral student. *Journal of Asian Pacific Communication, 15*(1), 153–170.

Li, Y. (2006a). Negotiating knowledge contribution to multiple discourse communities: A doctoral student of computer science writing for publication. *Journal of Second Language Writing, 15*(3), 159–178.

Li, Y. (2006b). A doctoral student of physics writing for publication: A sociopolitically-oriented case study. *English for Specific Purposes, 25*(4), 456–478.

Li, Y. (2007a). Apprentice scholarly writing in a community of practice: An intraview of an NNES graduate student writing a research article. *TESOL Quarterly, 41*(1), 55–79.

Li, Y. (2007b). Composing citations through language reuse: A doctoral student of biomedicine writing a research paper. *Asian Journal of English Language Teaching, 17*, 1–27.

Li, Y. (2014a). Seeking entry to the North American market: Chinese management academics publishing internationally. *Journal of English for Academic Purposes, 13*(1), 41–52.

Li, Y. (2014b). Chinese medical doctors negotiating the pressure of the publication requirement. *Ibérica, 28*, 107–128.

Li, Y., & Cargill, M. (2019). Observing and reflecting in an ERPP "master class": Learning and thinking about application. In J. Corcoran, K. Englander, & L. Muresan (Eds.), *Pedagogies and policies on publishing research in English: Local initiatives supporting international scholars* (pp. 143–160). London and New York: Routledge.

Li, Y., & Flowerdew, J. (2007). Shaping Chinese novice scientists' manuscripts for publication. *Journal of Second Language Writing, 16*(2), 100–117.

Li, Y., & Flowerdew, J. (2009). International engagement versus local commitment: Hong Kong academics in the humanities and social sciences writing for publication. *Journal of English for Academic Purposes, 8*(4), 279–293.

Li, Y., & Flowerdew, J. (2020). Teaching English for Research Publication Purposes (ERPP): A review of language teachers' pedagogical initiatives. *English for Specific Purposes, 49*, 29–41.

Li, Y., Flowerdew, J., & Cargill, M. (2018). Teaching English for research publication purposes to science students in China: A case study of an experienced teacher in the classroom. *Journal of English for Academic Purposes, 35*, 116–129.

Lillis, T. (2008). Ethnography as method, methodology, and "deep theorizing". *Written Communication, 2*(53), 353–388.

Lillis, T. (2012). Economies of signs in writing for academic publication: The case of English medium "national" journals. *Journal of Advanced Composition, 32*(3–4), 695–722.

Lillis, T., & Curry, M. J. (2010). *Academic writing in a global context: The politics and practices of publishing in English.* London: Routledge.

Lillis, T., & Curry, M. J. (2015). The politics of English, language and uptake: The case of international academic journal article reviews. *AILA Review, 28*, 127–150.

Lillis, T., & Scott, M. (2007). Defining academic literacies research: Issues of epistemology, ideology, and strategy. Special issue. New directions in academic literacies. *Journal of Applied Linguistics, 4*(1), 5–32.

Lin, L., & Evans, S. (2012). Structural patterns in empirical research articles: A cross-disciplinary study. *English for Specific Purposes, 31*, 150–160.

Lincoln, Y. S., & Guba, E. G. (1985). *Naturalistic inquiry*. Beverly Hills, CA: Sage Publications.

Liu, J. (2004). Co-constructing academic discourse from the periphery: Chinese applied linguists' centripetal participation in scholarly publication. *Asian Journal of English Language Teaching, 14*, 1–22.

Liu, L. A. (2014). Addressing reviewer comments as an integrative negotiation. *Management and Organization Review, 10*, 183–190.

Loi, C., Evans, M., Lim, J., & Akkakoson, S. (2016). A comparison between Malay and English research articled discussions: A move analysis. *SAGE Open, 6*(2), 1–11.

López-Navarro, I., Moreno, A., Quintanilla, M., & Rey-Rocha, J. (2015). Why do I publish research articles in English instead of my own language? Differences in Spanish researchers' motivations across scientific domains. *Scientometrics, 103*(3), 939–976.

Lorés-Sanz, R. (2004). On RA abstracts: From rhetorical structure to thematic organization. *English for Specific Purposes, 23*, 280–302.

Lorés-Sanz, R. (2016). ELF in the making? Simplification and hybridity in abstract writing. *Journal of English as a Lingua Franca, 5*(1), 53–81.

Lu, X., Casal, J. E., & Liu, Y. (2020). The rhetorical functions of syntactically complex sentences in social science research article introductions. *Journal of English for Academic Purposes, 44*, 100832. https://doi.org/10.1016/j.jeap.2019.100832

Luo, N., & Hyland, K. (2021). International publishing as a networked activity: Collegial support for Chinese scientists. *Applied Linguistics, 42*(1), 164–185.

Luzón, M. J. (2013). Public communication of science in blogs. *Written Communication, 30*(4), 428–457.

Luzón, M., & Pérez-Llantada, C. (Eds.). (2019). *Science communication on the Internet: Old genres meet new genres*. Amsterdam: John Benjamins Publishing Company.

Mack, C. (2012). Editorial: How to write a good scientific paper: Citations. *Journal of Micro/Nanolithography, MEMS, and MOEMS, 11*(3), 030101.

Maher, M. A, & Say, B. H. (2016). Doctoral supervisors as learners and teachers of disciplinary writing. In C. M. Badenhorst & C. Guerin (Eds.), *Research literacies and writing pedagogies for masters and doctoral writers* (pp. 277–294). Studies in writing series. Leiden, the Netherlands: Brill Publishing.

Martín, P., Rey-Rocha, J., Burgess, S., & Moreno, A. I. (2014). Publishing research in English-language journals: Attitudes, strategies and difficulties of multilingual scholars of medicine. *Journal of English for Academic Purposes, 16*, 57–67.

Martinez, R. (2018). 'Specially in the last years…': Evidence of ELF and non-native English forms in international journals. *Journal of English for Academic Purposes, 33*, 40–52.

Matarese, V. (2013). *Supporting research writing: Roles and challenges in multilingual settings* (1st ed.). Chandos information professional series. Oxford: Chandos Publishing.

Matarese, V. (2016). *Editing research: The author editing approach to providing effective support to writers of research papers*. Medford, OR: Information Today Inc.

Matzler, P. P. (2021). Grant proposal abstracts in science and engineering: A prototypical move-structure pattern and its variations. *Journal of English for Academic Purposes, 49*, 100938.

Mauranen, A., Hynninen, N., & Ranta, E. (2010). English as an academic lingua franca: The ELFA project. *English for Specific Purposes, 29*(3), 183–190.

McDougall-Waters, J., Moxham, N., & Fyfe, A. (2015). *Philosophical transactions: 350 years of publishing at the Royal Society (1665–2015)*. London: The Royal Society.

McDowell, L., & Liardét, C. L. F. (2019). Japanese materials scientists' experiences with English for research publication purposes. *Journal of English for Academic Purposes, 37*, 141–153.

McGrail, M. R., Rickard, C. M., & Jones, C. R. (2006). Publish or perish: A systematic review of interventions to increase academic publication rates. *Higher Education Research & Development, 25*(1), 19–35.

McGrath, L. (2016). Open-access writing: An investigation into the online drafting and revision of a research article in pure mathematics. *English for Specific Purposes, 43*, 25–36.

McIntosh, K., Connor, U., & Gopkinar-Shelton, E. (2017). What intercultural rhetoric can bring to EAP/ESP writing studies in an English as a lingua franca world. *Journal of English for Academic Purposes, 29*, 12–20.

McKinley, J., & Rose, H. (2018). Conceptualizations of language errors, standards, norms and nativeness in English for research publication purposes: An analysis of journal submission guidelines. *Journal of Second Language Writing, 42*, 1–11.

Meadows, A. J. (1985). The scientific paper as an archaeological artifact. *Journal of Information Science, 11*, 27–30.

Meneghini, R., & Packer, A. L. (2007). Is there science beyond English? *EMBO Reports, 8*, 112–116.

Messekher, H., & Miliani, M. (2019). Teaching the craft: From thesis writing to writing research for publication. In J. N. Corcoran, K. Englander, & L.-M. Muresan (Eds.), *Pedagogies and policies for publishing research in English: Local initiatives supporting international scholars* (pp. 195–214). New York and London: Routledge.

Michaels, D. (2006). Politicizing peer review: Scientific perspective. In W. Wagner & R. Steinzor (Eds.), *Rescuing science from politics: Regulation and the distortion of scientific research* (pp. 219–237). Cambridge: Cambridge University Press.

Milagros del Saz Rubio, M. (2011). A pragmatic approach to the macro-structure and metadiscoursal features of research article introductions in the field of Agricultural Sciences. *English for Specific Purposes, 30*(4), 258–271.

Monahan, T. (2011). Surveillance as cultural practice. *The Sociological Quarterly, 52*(4), 495–508.

Monteiro, K., & Hirano, E. (2020). A periphery inside a semi-periphery: The uneven participation of Brazilian scholars in the international community. *English for Specific Purposes, 58*, 15–29.

Moore, S. (2003). Writers' retreats for academics: Exploring and increasing the motivation to write. *Journal of Further and Higher Education, 27*(3), 333–342.

Morell, T. (2015). International conference paper presentation: A multimodal analysis to determine effectiveness. *English for Specific Purposes, 37*, 137–150.

Moreno, A. I., & Swales, J. M. (2018). Strengthening move analysis methodology towards bridging the function-form gap. *English for Specific Purposes, 50*, 40–63.

Morrison, W. M. (2019). *China's economic rise: History, trends, challenges, and implications for the United States*. Washington, DC: Congressional Research Service.

Motta-Roth, D. (1998). Discourse analysis and academic book reviews: A study of text and disciplinary cultures. In I. Fortanet, S. Posteguillo, J. C. Palmer, & J. F. Coll (Eds.), *Genre studies in English for academic purposes* (pp. 29–58). Castelló, Spain: Publicacions de la Universitat Jaume I.

Moxham, N., & Fyfe, A. (2017). The Royal Society and the prehistory of peer review 1665–1965. *The Historical Journal, 61*(4), 863–889.

Mu, C. (2020). *Understanding Chinese multilingual scholars' experiences of writing and publishing in English: A social-cognitive perspective*. Cham, Switzerland: Palgrave Macmillan.

Mungra, P., & Webber, P. (2010). Peer review process in medical research publications: Language and content comments. *English for Specific Purposes, 29*, 43–53.

Mur Dueñas, P. (2012). Getting research published internationally in English: An ethnographic account of a team of Finance Spanish scholars' struggles. *Ibérica, 24*, 139–156.

Mur-Dueñas, P. (2019). The experience of a NNES Outer Circle novice scholar in scholarly publication. In P. Habibie & K. Hyland (Eds.), *Novice writers and scholarly publication: Authors, mentors, gatekeepers* (pp. 97–115). Basingstoke: Palgrave Macmillan.

Muresan, L. M., & Pérez-Llantada, C. (2014). English for research publication and dissemination in bi-/multiliterate environments: The case of Romanian academics. *Journal of English for Academic Purposes, 13*, 53–64.

Murray, R. (2013). *Writing for academic journals* (3rd ed.). Maidenhead: Open University Press.

Murray, R., & Newton, M. (2008). Facilitating writing for publication. *Physiotherapy, 94*(1), 29–34.

Murray, R., & Newton, M. (2009). Writing retreat as structured intervention: Margin or mainstream? *Higher Education Research and Development, 28*, 541–553.

Murray, R., Thow, M., Moore, S., & Murphy, M. (2008). The writing consultation: Developing academic writing practices. *Journal of Further and Higher Education, 32*(2), 119–128.

Myers, G. (1989). The pragmatics of politeness in scientific articles. *Applied Linguistics, 10*(1), 1–35.

Myers, G. (1990). *Writing biology: Texts in the social construction of scientific knowledge*. Madison, WI: University of Wisconsin Press.

Na, L., & Hyland, K. (2019). "I won't publish in Chinese now": Publishing, translation and the non-English speaking academic. *Journal of English for Academic Purposes, 39*. 37–47.

Negretti, R., & McGrath, L. (2018). Scaffolding genre knowledge and metacognition: Insights from an L2 doctoral research writing course. *Journal of Second Language Writing, 40*, 12–31.

Negretti, R., & McGrath, L. (2020). English for specific playfulness? How doctoral students in Science, Technology, Engineering and Mathematics manipulate genre. *English for Specific Purposes, 60*, 26–39.

Nickerson, R. S. (1998). Confirmation bias: A ubiquitous phenomenon in many guises. *Review of General Psychology, 2*(2), 175–220.

Nunan, D. (2004). *Task-based language teaching*. Cambridge: Cambridge University Press.

Nwogu, K. N. (1997). The medical research paper: Structure and functions. *English for Specific Purposes (New York), 16*(2), 119–138.

O'Malley, B. (2016, January 29). Coimbra Group tells U-Multirank to revamp its data. *University World News*. Retrieved from www.universityworldnews.com/post.php?story=20160130004207648

Odell, L., Goswami, D., & Harrington, A. (1983). The discourse-based interview: A procedure for exploring the tacit knowledge of writers in nonacademic settings. In P. Mosenthal, L. Tamor, & S. A. Walmsley (Eds.), *Research on writing: Principles and methods* (pp. 221–236). New York: Longman.

Okamura, A. (2006). Two types of strategies used by Japanese scientists, when writing research articles in English. *System, 34*(1), 68–79.

Oswald, E., & Grosjean, S. (2004). Confirmation bias. In R. F. Pohl (Ed.), *Cognitive illusions: A handbook on fallacies and biases in thinking, judgement and memory* (pp. 79–96). Hove: Psychology Press.

Oswald, N. (2009, April 2). Does Your h-index Measure Up? Retrieved from https://bitesizebio.com/13614/does-your-h-index-measure-up/

Paltridge, B. (2012). *Discourse analysis: An introduction* (2nd ed.). London: Continuum.

Paltridge, B. (2013). Referees' comments on submissions to peer-reviewed journals: When is a suggestion not a suggestion? *Studies in Higher Education, 40*(1), 106–122.

Paltridge, B. (2015). Language, identity, and communities of practice. In D. N. Djenar, A. Mahboob, & K. Cruickshank (Eds.), *Language and identity across modes of communication* (pp. 15–25). Berlin: Mouton de Gruyter.

Paltridge, B. (2016). Writing retreats as writing pedagogy. *Writing & Pedagogy, 8*(1), 199–213.

Paltridge, B. (2017). *The discourse of peer review: Reviewing submissions to academic journals.* London: Palgrave Macmillan.

Paltridge, B. (2019a). Looking inside the world of peer review: Implications for graduate student writers. *Language Teaching, 52*(3), 331–342.

Paltridge, B. (2019b). Reviewers' feedback on second language writers' submissions to academic journals. In K. Hyland & F. Hyland (Eds.), *Feedback in second language writing: Contexts and issues* (pp. 226–243). Cambridge: Cambridge University Press.

Paltridge, B. (2020a). Engagement and reviewers' reports on submissions to academic journals. *Journal of English for Research Publication Purposes, 1,* 4–27.

Paltridge, B. (2020b). Writing for academic journals in the digital era. *RELC Journal, 51*(1), 147–157.

Paltridge, B., & Starfield, S. (2016). *Getting published in academic journals: Navigating the publication process.* Ann Arbor, MI: University of Michigan.

Paltridge, B., & Starfield, S. (2020). *Thesis and dissertation writing in a second language: A handbook for students and their supervisors* (2nd ed.). London: Routledge.

Paltridge, B., Starfield, S., & Tardy, C. (2016). *Ethnographic perspectives on academic writing.* Oxford: Oxford University Press.

Paré, A. (2010). Stop the presses: Concerns about premature publication. In C. Aitchison, B. Kamler, & A. Lee (Eds.), *Publishing pedagogies for the doctorate and beyond* (pp. 30–46). London and New York: Routledge.

Paré, A. (2011). Speaking of writing: Supervisory feedback and the dissertation. In L. McAlpine & C. Amundsen (Eds.), *Doctoral education: Research-based strategies for doctoral students, supervisors and administrators* (pp. 59–74). New York: Springer.

Parker, R. (2009). A learning community approach to doctoral education in the social sciences. *Teaching in Higher Education, 14*(1), 43–54.

Patel, V., & Kim, Y. R. (2007). Contribution of low- and middle-income countries to research published in leading general psychiatry journals, 2002–2004. *British Journal of Psychiatry, 190,* 77–78.

Peacock, M. (2002). Communicative moves in the discussion section of research articles. *System, 30*(4), 479–497.

Pennycook, A. (1994). *The cultural politics of English as an international language.* Harlow: Longman Group UK.

Pennycook, A. (1998). *English and the discourses of colonialism.* London and New York: Routledge.

Pennycook, A. (2000). English, politics, ideology: From colonial celebration to postcolonial performativity. In T. Ricento (Ed.), *Ideology, politics, and language policies: Focus on English* (pp. 107–119). Amsterdam: John Benjamins.

Pérez-Llantada, C. (2014). *Scientific discourse and the rhetoric of globalisation.* London: Bloomsbury.

Pérez-Llantada, C. (2015). Genres in the forefront, languages in the background: The scope of genre analysis in language-related scenarios. *Journal of English for Academic Purposes, 19*(25), 10–21.

Pérez-Llantada, C. (2016). How is the digital medium shaping research genres? Some cross-disciplinary trends. *ESP Today, 4*(1), 22–42.

Pérez-Llantada, C., Plo, R., & Ferguson, G. (2011). "You don't say what you know, only what you can": The perceptions and practices of senior Spanish academics regarding research dissemination in English. *English for Specific Purposes, 30*(1), 18–30.

Petric, B. (2014). English-medium journals in Serbia: Editors' perspectives. In K. Bennett (Ed.), *The semiperiphery of academic writing: Discourses, communities and practices* (pp. 189–209). Basingstoke: Palgrave Macmillan.

Philips, T. (2013). Tutor training and services for multilingual graduate writers: A reconsideration. *Praxis: A Writing Center Journal, 10*(2).

Philips, T. (2016). Writing center support for graduate students: An integrated model. In S. Simpson et al. (Eds.), *Supporting graduate student writers* (pp. 159–170). Ann Arbor, MI: University of Michigan Press.

Phillipson, R. (1992). *Linguistic imperialism*. Oxford: Oxford University Press.

Phillipson, R. (2008). Lingua franca or lingua frankensteinia? English in European integration and globalisation. *World Englishes, 27*(2), 250–267.

Phillipson, R. (2009). *Linguistic imperialism continued*. London: Routledge.

Phillipson, R., & Skutnabb-Kangas, T. S. (1994). English, panacea or pandemic. *Sociolinguistica*, 1–12.

Politzer-Ahles, S., Holliday, J. J., Girolamo, T., Spychalska, M., & Harper Berkson, K. (2017). Is linguistic injustice a myth? A response to Hyland (2016). *Journal of Second Language Writing, 34*, 3–8.

Pratt, M. (1991). Arts of the contact zone. *Profession*, 33–40.

Pronskikh, V. (2018). Linguistic privilege and justice: What can we learn from STEM? *Philosophical Papers: Linguistic Justice and Analytic Philosophy, 47*(1), 71–92.

Purdy, J. P. (2014). What can design thinking offer writing studies? *College Composition and Communication, 65*, 612–641.

Ramirez-Castaneda, V. (2020). Disadvantages in preparing and publishing scientific papers caused by the dominance of the English language in science: The case of Colombian researchers in biological sciences. *PLoS ONE, 15*(9), e0238372.

Rawat, S., & Meena, S. (2014). Publish or perish: Where are we heading? *Journal of Research in Medical Sciences, 19*(2), 87–89.

Riazi, A. M., Ghanbar, H., & Fazel, I. (2020). The contexts, theoretical and methodological orientation of EAP research: Evidence from empirical articles published in the *Journal of English for Academic Purposes. Journal of English for Academic Purposes, 48*, 1–17.

Ribeiro, L. C., Rapini, M. S., Alves Silva, L., & Alburquerque, E. M. (2018). Growth patterns of the network of international collaboration in science. *Scientometrics, 114*(1), 159–179.

Ricento, T. (Ed.). (2000). *Ideology, politics, and language policies: Focus on English*. Amsterdam: John Benjamins.

Robertson, R. (1992). *Globalization: Social theory and global culture*. London: Sage.

Rohra, D. K. (2011). Representation of less-developed countries in pharmacology journals: An online survey of corresponding authors. *BMC Medical Research Methodology, 11*(60), 160–165.

Root-Bernstein, M., & Ladle, R. J. (2014). Multilinguismo nas ciências ambientais: Ahora ya! [Multilingualism in environmental sciences: It's about time!]. *Ambio, 43*, 836–837.

Ross, J., Hill, K., Egilman, D., & Krumholz, H. (2008). Guest authorship and ghostwriting in publications related to Rofecoxib: A case study of industry documents from Rofecoxib Litigation. *JAMA: The Journal of the American Medical Association, 299*(15), 1800–1812.

Rowley-Jolivet, E. (2002). Visual discourse in scientific conference papers: A genre-based study. *English for Specific Purposes, 21*, 19–40.

Rowley-Jolivet, E. (2012). Oralising text slides in scientific conference presentations: A multimodal corpus analysis. In A. Boulton, S. Carter-Thomas, & E. Rowley-Jolivet (Eds.), *Corpus-informed research and learning in ESP* (pp. 137–165). Amsterdam: John Benjamins.

Rowley-Jolivet, E., & Carter-Thomas, S. (2005a). The rhetoric of conference presentation introductions: Context, argument, and interaction. *International Journal of Applied Linguistics, 15*(1), 45–70.

Rowley-Jolivet, E., & Carter-Thomas, S. (2005b). Genre awareness and rhetorical appropriacy: Manipulation of information structure by NS and NNS scientists in the international conference setting. *English for Specific Purposes, 24*(1), 41–64.

Rozycki, W., & Johnson, N. H. (2013). Non-canonical grammar in Best Paper award winners in engineering. *English for Specific Purposes, 20,* 89–100.

Ryazanova, O., McNamara, P., & Aguinis, H. (2017). Research performance as a quality signal in international labor markets: Visibility of business schools worldwide through a global research performance system. *Journal of World Business, 52*(6), 831–841.

Salager-Meyer, F. (2008). Scientific publishing in developing countries: Challenges for the future. *Journal of English for Academic Purposes, 7*(2), 121–132.

Salager-Meyer, F. (2010). Academic book reviews and the construction of scientific knowledge (1890–2005). In M. L. Gea Valor, I. García Izquierdo, & M. J. Esteve (Eds.), *Linguistic and translation studies in scientific communication* (pp. 39–68). Bern, Switzerland: Peter Lang.

Salager-Meyer, F. (2014). Writing and publishing in peripheral scholarly journals: How to enhance the global influence of multilingual scholars? *Journal of English for Academic Purposes, 13*(1), 78–82.

Salager-Meyer, F. (2015). Peripheral scholarly journals: From locality to globality. *Ibérica, 30,* 15–36.

Salager-Meyer, F., Alcaraz Ariza, M. A., & Pabón Berbesí, M. (2007). Collegiality, critique and the construction of scientific argumentation in medical book reviews: A diachronic approach. *Journal of Pragmatics, 39,* 1758–1774.

Salmani Nodoushan, M. A., & Montazeran, H. (2012). The book review genre: A structural move analysis. *International Journal of Language Studies, 6*(1), 1–30.

Samraj, B. (2016). Discourse structure and variation in manuscript reviews: Implications for genre categorisation. *English for Specific Purposes, 42,* 76–88.

Sancho Guinda, C. (2015). Genres on the move: Currency and erosion of the genre moves construct. *Journal of English for Academic Purposes, 19,* 73–87.

Saposnik, G., Ovbiagele, B., Raptis, S., Fisher, M., & Johnston, S. C. (2014). Effect of English proficiency and research funding on acceptance of submitted articles to "Stroke" journal. *Stroke, 45,* 1862–1868.

Schofer, E., & Meyer, J. W. (2005), The worldwide expansion of higher education in the twentieth century. *American Sociological Review, 70*(6), 898–920.

Schultz, D. M. (2009). *The process of publishing scientific papers. Eloquent science: A practical guide to becoming a better writer, speaker, and atmospheric scientist.* Boston, MA: American Meteorological Society.

Selinker, L., Tarone, E., & Hanzeli, V. (Eds.). (1981). *English for academic and technical purposes: Studies in honor of Louis Trimble.* Rowley, MA: Newbury House.

Shapin, S. (1984). Pump and circumstance: Robert Boyle's literary technology. *Social Studies of Science, 14*(4), 481–520.

Shapin, S., & Schaffer, S. (1985). *Leviathan and the air-pump: Hobbes, Boyle, and the experimental life.* Princeton, NJ: Princeton University Press.

Shchemeleva, I. (2021). "There's no discrimination, these are just the rules of the game": Russian scholars' perception of the research writing and publication process in English. *Publications, 9*(1), 8.

Sheldon, E. (2018). Dialogic spaces of knowledge construction in research articles: Conclusion sections written by English L1, English L2 and Spanish L1 writers. *Ibérica, 35,* 13–40.

Sheridan, C. L. (2015). National journals and centering institutions: A historiography of an English language teaching journal in Taiwan. *English for Specific Purposes, 38*, 70–84.

Shi, L. (2003). Writing in two cultures: Chinese professors return from the west. *The Canadian Modern Language Review, 59*, 369–391.

Shvidko, E., & Atkinson, D. (2019). From student to scholar: Making the leap to writing for publication. In P. Habibie & K. Hyland (Eds.), *Novice writers and scholarly publication. Authors, mentors, gatekeepers* (pp. 155–177). Cham, Switzerland: Palgrave Macmillan.

Siemens, G. (2005). Connectivism: A learning theory for the digital age. *International Journal of Instructional Technology & Distance Learning, 2*(1).

Soler, J., & Cooper, A. (2017). 'We have learned your paper': Academic inequality and the discourse of parasite publishers (Tilburg Papers in Culture Studies; No. 184).

Spier, R. (2002). The history of the peer-review process. *Trends in Biotechnology, 20*(8), 357–358.

St. John, M. J. (1987). Writing processes of Spanish scientists publishing in English. *English for Specific Purposes, 6*, 113–120.

Starfield, S., & Paltridge, B. (2019). Journal editors: Gatekeepers or custodians? In P. Habibie & K. Hyland (Eds.), *Novice writers and scholarly publication: Authors, mentors, gatekeepers* (pp. 253–270). Cham, Switzerland: Palgrave Macmillan.

Statista. (2020). The 20 countries with the largest gross domestic product (GDP) in 2020. Retrieved from www.statista.com/statistics/268173/countries-with-the-largest-gross-domestic-product-gdp/

Steen, R. G. (2011). Retractions in the scientific literature: Is the incidence of research fraud increasing? *Journal of Medical Ethics, 37*(4), 249–253.

Stockemer, D., & Wigginton, M. J. (2019). Publishing in English or another language: An inclusive study of scholar's language publication preferences in the natural, social and interdisciplinary sciences. *Scientometrics, 118*(2), 645–652.

Stoller, F. L., & Robinson, M. S. (2013). Chemistry journal articles: An interdisciplinary approach to move analysis with pedagogical aims. *English for Specific Purposes (New York), 32*(1), 45–57.

Storch, N. (2013). *Collaborative writing in L2 classrooms.* Bristol: Multilingual Matters.

Stotesbury, H. (2003). Evaluation in research article abstracts in the narrative and hard sciences. *Journal of English for Academic Purposes, 2*, 327–341.

Strauss, P. (2019). Shakespeare and the English poets: The influence of native speaking English reviewers on the acceptance of journal articles. *Publications, 7*(1), 20.

Sudhira, H. S. (2018, January 28). The precarious prevalence of predatory journals. *Research Matters.* Retrieved from https://researchmatters.in/news/precarious-prevalence-predatory-journals

Swales, J. M. (1990). *Genre analysis: English in academic and research settings.* Cambridge: Cambridge University Press.

Swales, J. M. (1997). English as 'Tyrannosaurus Rex'. *World Englishes, 16*, 373–382.

Swales, J. M. (2004). *Research genres: Exploration and application.* Cambridge, UK: Cambridge University Press.

Swales, J. M. (2019). Envoi. In J. Corcoran, K. Englander, & L. Muresan (Eds.), *Pedagogies and policies on publishing research in English: Local initiatives supporting international scholars* (pp. 284–290). London and New York: Routledge.

Swales, J. M., & Feak, C. B. (2000). *English in today's research world: A writing guide.* Ann Arbor, MI: University of Michigan Press.

Swales, J. M., & Feak, C. B. (2012). *Academic writing for graduate students: Essential tasks and skills.* Ann Arbor, MI: University of Michigan Press.

Tardy, C. (2004). The role of English in scientific communication: Lingua franca or Tyrannosaurus Rex? *Journal of English for Academic Purposes, 3*, 247–269.

Tardy, C. M. (2005). It's like a story: Rhetorical knowledge development in advanced academic literacy. *Journal of English for Academic Purposes, 4*, 325–338.

Tardy, C. M. (2009). *Building genre knowledge.* West Lafayette, IN: Parlor Press.

Tarone, E., Dwyer, S., Gillette, S., & Icke, V. (1998). On the use of the passive and active voice in astrophysics journal papers: With extensions to other languages and other fields. *English for Specific Purposes, 17*(1), 113–132.

Thatcher, A., Zhang, M., Todoroski, H., Chau, A., Wang, J., & Liang, G. (2020). Predicting the impact of COVID-19 on Australian universities. *Journal of Risk and Financial Management, 13*, 188.

Thomson, P., & Kamler, B. (2013). *Writing for peer reviewed journals: Strategies for getting published.* London: Routledge.

Thorne, S. L., & Reinhardt, J. (2008). Bridging activities, new media literacies: And advanced foreign language proficiency. *CALICO Journal, 25*, 558–572.

Tomkins, A., Zhang, M., & Heavlin, W. (2017). Reviewer bias in single- versus double-blind peer review. (Report). *Proceedings of the National Academy of Sciences of the United States, 114*(48), 12708–12713.

Trowler, P., Saunders, M., & Bamber, V. (2012). *Tribes and territories in the 21st century: Rethinking the significance of disciplines in higher education.* Abingdon, UK: Routledge.

Tscharntke, T., Hochberg, M. E., Rand, T. A., Resh, V. H., & Krauss, J. (2007). Author sequence and credit for contributions in multiauthored publications. *PLoS Biology, 5*(1), e18.

Tse, P., & Hyland, K. (2008). 'Robot kung fu': Gender and the performance of a professional identity. *Journal of Pragmatics, 40*(7), 1232–1248.

Tseng, M. (2011). The genre of research grant proposals: Towards a cognitive–pragmatic analysis. *Journal of Pragmatics, 43*, 2254–2268.

Turner, J. (2011). Rewriting writing in higher education: The contested spaces of proofreading. *Studies in Higher Education, 36*, 427–440.

Tusting, T., McCulloch, S., Bhatt, I., Hamilton, M., & Barton, D. (2019). *Academics writing: The dynamics of knowledge creation.* New York: Routledge.

Üsdiken, B. (2014). Centres and peripheries: Research styles and publication patterns in 'top' US journals and their European alternatives, 1960–2010. *Journal of Management Studies, 51*(5), 764–789.

Usher, E. (2017, February 3). Four megatrends in tertiary educations: massification. Retrieved from https://higheredstrategy.com/four-megatrends-in-international-higher-education-massification/

Uysal, H. H. (2014). Turkish academic culture in transition: Centre-based state policies and semiperipheral practices of research, publishing and promotion. In K. Bennett (Ed.), *The semiperiphery of academic writing: Discourses, communities and practices* (pp. 165–188). Basingstoke: Palgrave Macmillan

Valero, A., & Van Reenen, J. (2016). How universities boost economic growth. Retrieved from https://voxeu.org/article/how-universities-boost-economic-growth

Van Dijk, T. A. (1994). Academic nationalism [Editorial]. *Discourse and Society, 5*, 275–276.

Van Parijs, P. (2004). Europe's linguistic challenge. *Archives Européennes de Sociologie, 45*(1), 113–154.

Van Parijs, P. (2007). Tackling the Anglophones' free ride. Fair linguistic cooperation with a global lingua franca. *AILA Review, 20*(1), 72–78.

Vandergriff, I. (2016). *Second-language discourse in the digital world: Linguistic and social practices in and beyond the networked classroom.* Amsterdam: John Benjamins.

Vanman, E., Paul, B., Ito, T., & Miller, N. (1997). The modern face of prejudice and structural features that moderate the effect of cooperation on affect. *Journal of Personality and Social Psychology, 73*(5), 941–959.

Vuong, Q. H. (2020). The limitations of retraction notices and the heroic acts of authors who correct the scholarly record: An analysis of retractions of papers published from 1975 to 2019. *Learned Publishing, 33,* 119–130.

Wallerstein, I. (1974). *The modern world-system* (2 volumes). New York and London: Academic Press.

Wallerstein, I. (2004). *World-systems analysis: An introduction.* Durham, NC: Duke University Press.

Ware, M., & Mabe, M. (2012). *The STM report* (3rd ed.). The Hague, the Netherlands: International Association of Scientific, Technical and Medical Publishers.

Ware, P., Kern, R., & Warschauer, M. (2016). The development of digital literacies. In R. M. Manchón & P. K. Matsuda (Eds.), *Handbook of second and foreign language writing* (pp. 307–328). Boston, MA: De Gruyter.

Warschauer, M., & Grimes, D. (2007). Audience, authorship, and artifact: The emergent semiotics of Web 2.0. *Annual Review of Applied Linguistics, 27,* 1–23.

Watson-Gegeo, K. A. (1988). Ethnography in ESL: Defining the essentials. *TESOL Quarterly, 22*(4), 575–592.

Weber, E. (1992). *Movements, currents, trends: Aspects of European thought in the nineteenth and twentieth centuries.* Lexington, MA: D.C. Heath.

Williams, I. A. (1999). Results sections of medical research articles: Analysis of rhetorical categories for pedagogical purposes. *English for Specific Purposes, 18*(4), 347–366.

Wood, A. (2001). International scientific English. In J. Flowerdew & M. Peacock (Eds.), *Research perspectives on English for academic purposes* (pp. 71–83). Cambridge: Cambridge University Press.

Wulff, S., Swales, J. M., & Keller, K. (2009). "We have about seven minutes for questions": The discussion sessions from a specialized conference. *English for Specific Purposes, 28,* 79–92.

Xu, J. (2020). Guest post — How China's new policy may change researchers' publishing behavior. Retrieved from https://scholarlykitchen.sspnet.org/2020/03/03/guest-post-how-chinas-new-policy-may-change-researchers-publishing-behavior/

INDEX